MIDDLE EASTERN COOKERY

BY EVA ZANE

DRAWINGS & ANNOTATIONS
BY KEITH HALONEN

101 PRODUCTIONS
SAN FRANCISCO
1974

TO THE WOMEN OF THESE LANDS
WHOSE HOSPITALITY KNOWS NO BOUNDARIES

And to the many friends and relatives who made this book a reality:
Coralie and Al Castle for their long hours of editorial assistance;
my sister Sue Banducci for her support;
and those who helped with research and offered me their recipes
and kitchens for endless testing—Henry Younger, Jeannie Fritch,
Rita and Ray Martin, John Dratos, the Tatarianis, the Dolbergs, Helen
Nichols, Fran Chronis, Nitsa of the Israeli Tourist office of Los Angeles,
Clementine of the Greek tourist office of Los Angeles and
those I have specifically thanked in the text of various recipes;
and lastly to Tina, Byron and Dino, my three epicurean children.

Third Printing, November, 1977

Copyright © 1974 by Eva Zane
Drawings © 1974 by Keith Halonen

Printed in the United States of America

Distributed to the book trade in the United States by
Charles Scribner's Sons, New York

Published by 101 Productions
834 Mission Street, San Francisco, California 94103

Library of Congress Cataloging in Publication Data

Zane, Eva.
    Middle Eastern cookery.

    1.   Cookery, Near East.   I.   Title.
TX725.N36Z36   641.5'956   74-18088
ISBN 0-912238-51-8
ISBN 0-912238-50-X (pbk.)

CONTENTS

OMAR AND THE HOURI

THE MIDDLE EAST AND ITS CUISINES

THIS IS a book of poetry—the poetry of the Middle East and its swirling deserts, rugged mountains, and far too few fertile plains; its rivers and seas; its peoples. Here the remnants of glorious ancient civilizations are trying new ways to wrest a living from soil that has been depleted by centuries of over-cultivation, newly determined to regain their place in the sun.

Being a Greek I have long felt a kinship to the peoples of these neighboring lands. When I conceived this book and began my research, I soon became engrossed in the panorama of their history. I was mesmerized by myriad visions of layer upon layer of mystical past civilizations, each like a Persian rug of colorful, intricate patterns in architecture, religions, traditions, customs and, of course, foods. Verse is not needed to describe the Middle East. Its very existence, past and present, can excite pleasure by beautiful, imaginative, and elevated thoughts—the pure poetry of a spectacular view.

Embark with me on an imaginative culinary adventure, traveling by magic carpet from the time when civilization was in its cradle to the present—from the Afghanistan border to the Atlantic shores of Morocco. We'll explore an area defined more by its history and cultures than by its geography. We'll taste foods that are far more than mere sustenance—foods that are a way of life, often intimately involved in religion; foods that have caused great conflicts, that have influenced economic, social, and political theory and played a role in the development of science and technology, medicine and the arts; foods that are an integral part of the folklore and traditions of ethnic groups almost as numberless as grains of sand in a desert.

I cannot be presumptuous enough to attempt a detailed history of these shifting peoples and their cultures as they were blown by wild, turbulent winds of war, slavery, tyranny and religion, as many were destroyed by famine, drought and plague. However, a few broad strokes of the brush may serve to explain how dynamic oases of fertility and knowledge brought civilization to a predominantly desolate land.

Since the beginning of time, water has been the key to life. Nowhere is this more dramatically demonstrated than in the arid Middle East where so much of the land consists of rocky mountains, hot

THE MIDDLE EAST

oceans of sand, sparsely vegetated hills and high plateaus suitable only for limited grazing. For people choosing to live in these areas, foraging for food has always been a struggle. Grazing animals that could be herded from place to place helped by converting the scattered grasses into meat and milk for human nourishment. Many wandering tribes of nomads still choose this way of life, though today they may supplement their meat and milk with grain, vegetables, fruit, sweets and coffee.

In ages past, thousands of warlike wanderers found better things to fight for than possession of barren wastes. Fertile river valleys and seacoasts seemed ripe for the picking, and history records wave after wave of hungry peoples sweeping in to conquer, settle and enjoy a better life. They are credited with popularizing not only meat, but also an amazing variety of cheeses. Milk quickly soured in the heat and was not easily transported, yet it was too precious a food to throw away. No one knows when the thick milk of the ewe, the nanny goat, the mare, the jenny and the camel was first stored in a butchered animal's stomach for transporting to the next campsite; or when the first palate found that fermented curds, with a unique flavor imparted by such containers, were a great delicacy. But discovering the keeping qualities of milk in the form of cheese—the harder the better—can be ranked with drying, salting and freezing in man's successful defiance of space and time when it comes to food. Unlike camels, which carry with them a reserve of fat in their humps to be metabolized later into energy and water, man has always depended on exterior ways to store and transport food for lean days.

Had life everywhere been as difficult as it was in the deserts of sand and salt, or in the mountains and high plateaus, Western civilization might never have been born. Most of man's energies might have been consumed in keeping alive, with none left for conceiving and building imposing edifices with their decorative statues, paintings, tapestries, rugs and furniture. There might have been little time to develop a written language, little time to contemplate the nature of man and his place in the universe.

Luckily, Nature in the Middle East was kind in a limited way. Rains from remote highlands flowed in rivers to the seas, bringing life-giving moisture and nutriments to portions of the deserts. Moisture separated by evaporation from the salt of the seas dropped along coastal areas. Man found he could plant vegetation and improve its food value by design instead of waiting for Nature to take its course, that he could fish and till, cultivate, harvest, store and cook food even better by fashioning tools and implements. With his tools he learned to divert rivers with dams, tunnels, pipes and canals and spread the precious water to grow food in areas Nature had neglected. In the process he found time to plan, philosophize, improve his comforts and, unfortunately, to connive. Wars made the fruits of other men's labors available to the powerful. To produce new wealth, conquered peoples were enslaved and exploited like tools and animals.

There is evidence that Stone Age man lived along the Jordan River as far back as 100,000 B.C. and that farming and fishing were pursued on the east coast of the Mediterranean at least 7,000 years ago. By 4000 B.C., olive trees were cultivated, not the prickly, scrubby variety with tiny fruit, but larger thornless trees that bore fleshy, thin-skinned drupes, loaded with precious oil for food, lighting, medicine and annointing the body. These trees grew well on hot, dry hills, in barren soil leached of nutriments by

WHERE JESUS PLAYED

centuries of erosion or over-cultivation. Unlike most nut and fruit trees, the olive survives for hundreds of years—some of today's trees date back to the time of Christ. Olives are a tremendous source of digestible, edible, energy-producing fats, so important in areas where animals are scarce. Little wonder that olives became a staple throughout the Middle East, either whole, or in the form of oil for salads and cooking.

It was around 4000 B.C., too, that tribes of unknown race arrived from the north or northeast to settle in the lush "Garden of Eden" where the Tigris and Euphrates had laid down thick layers of productive soil and kept them moist for growing grain and other crops. Perhaps it was the new energies of the interlopers combined with the agricultural knowledge of more placid peoples that gave birth to civilization in this nurturing "cradle." Here during the next 1000 years cuneiform writing and the Semitic languages (Hebrew, Arabic and others) had their start. The Semites expanded their influence westward to populous Palestine, Phoenicia, and Assyria; Egyptians and nomads to the south and east were brushed by their culture.

Meanwhile a mighty river system, flooding down each year from African mountain lakes over 4,000 winding miles away, was constantly depositing rich new silt along its lower valley and spreading black gold in a giant delta at its mouth on the Mediterranean Sea. Here the soil could never be depleted, for it was regenerated every year. As early as 5000 B.C. farmers were planting crops in the Nile Valley, and by 3000 B.C. its Caucasoid peoples had established a mighty civilization that was conquered only after 2500 years of triumph and glory. Hieroglyphics carved in stone and hieratic script on both leather and papyrus record epics of ancient King-Gods and their priests who governed the people.

Ousir, or Osiris, symbolizing the river that rises and falls, was at first a nature god embodying the spirit of vegetation that dies with the harvest to be reborn when the newly planted grain sprouts. As a king, he reputedly abolished cannibalism and taught his half-savage subjects how to fashion agricultural implements and how to produce grain and grapes for bread, beer and wine.

"Egypt" is the Greek name for the country of the Nile. Its own people first called their land Kemet, or "black," after the rich soil of the delta. Early language, a mixture of Semitic and Hamitic (North African) words, died 1000 years ago, except for modern use in the Coptic church. However, early concepts in geometry, surgery and astronomy, the 365-day calendar, and the importance of women in society have proved more durable. For the common people, daily meals comprised barley bread, fish, onions and beer with occasional fruit, meat and wine on holidays. The wealthy, with slaves to serve them, enjoyed fancy breads and cakes. Fertile fields yielded two to three crops of emmer wheat, beans, cabbages, cucumbers, lettuce, peas, onions, radishes, melons and fruits, and provided food for cattle, donkeys, geese, ducks, goats and sheep. Preservation of fish and meat by salting and drying, like the storing of grain, helped level the cycles of feast and famine.

That much of the art of cooking preceded widespread cultivation of various grains seems evident from the fact that raw grain is indigestible and its tight bran layers and husks are hard to remove. Without efficient milling methods, ancient Egyptians learned to roast the kernels on hot stones to loosen their unpalatable covers and in the process make them edible. The still-hard kernels could then be softened or even sprouted in water and fashioned into globs of dough to be transported and freshly baked into flat bread as needed (the bread itself kept poorly and quickly became hard and stale). The roasted kernels could also be turned into a somewhat less tasty gruel by mixing with extra water.

The first brewer of beer may well have been a careless cook who left her gruel in an open pot exposed to yeast spores drifting in the hot Egyptian air. Her consternation at seeing the gruel bubbling in the sun may have turned to interest as she tasted it and found a new flavor. And her interest may have heightened to excitement as she consumed the entire bowl and discovered a strange warmth flooding her veins. Semi-cooked bread fermented in water was found to produce an even better beverage.

That beer came before leavened bread can be argued on the basis that heat destroys the elasticity of gluten, the tenacious protein substance found chiefly in wheat, not other grains. After wheat strains were developed with looser bran coats and hulls that could be threshed off without roasting, one can imagine another forgetful cook staring in surprise at a neglected glob of dough that had blown up like a balloon. Here the yeast spores formed the same carbon dioxide bubbles, but the rubbery gluten entrapped them. Baking hardened the gluten and set the loaf in a light, fluffy form that kept much better. Leavened bread and cakes soon captured the attention of the upper classes. The new wheat remained rare and expensive for decades, perhaps centuries, but leavened bread enjoyed wide favor everywhere once such wheat became readily available and special yeasts, more efficient than the random types floating in the air, were produced. The brewing of beer and other fermentation of fruits and grains, of course, has long since become a major pursuit of science and technology.

The third millenium B.C. in the Middle East started with Canaanites migrating into southern Palestine from Arabian deserts and was marked not only by vast expansion of man's knowledge, but also by great fears of a multitude of angry gods. Religious sacrifices of animals and fellow humans were common. They were thought to be necessary to mollify particular deities controlling every facet of life—birth, health, marriage and death; sun, moon, sky, earth and water; hearth, home and food. Rulers were worshipped like gods; gods were deemed to possess all the many human foibles. The history of this period remains sketchy, for many peoples with intricate spoken vocabularies had no written language. Others, like the Phoenicians, wrote their early phonetic characters (later taught to the Greeks) on papyrus which soon crumbled.

It was around 2000 B.C. that Middle Eastern history became more hectic. Aryans from the Asian steppes moved into Persia. Hittites from Europe or Central Asia arrived in Asia Minor. In the southern Tigris-Euphrates valley the Babylonians became powerful and for a while dominated the warlike Assyrians to their north. Abraham migrated from Babylonia to Palestine to start the Hebrew culture with a revolutionary new religion to better serve man's needs—a single Divine Presence more sympathetic to man than the trivial, angry gods of the Egyptians. The Phoenician worshippers of many *baals* (deities) taught the Hebrews how to build temples. It wasn't long before the age of metals produced more efficient tools for fashioning stone and wood into vehicles, ships, temples and works of art and for better tilling of the soil

THE MIDDLE EAST

and harvesting of crops. Communication and trade expanded, bringing rice, sugarcane and spices from the Orient to the Middle East.

But man sorely needed Divine help, for there were many who used new tools and knowledge to destroy as well as to build, to massacre as well as to create. Seesaw power struggles became the order of the day in the Middle East and have continued ever since. At times small city-states predominated, but better remembered are the mighty empires: the Persian in 500 B.C., Alexander the Great in 300 B.C., the Roman around the time of Christ, the Byzantine starting in 300 A.D., Ottoman Turks from the 1500's to World War I. To me, the most fascinating empire of all is the dynamic one fashioned by the Arabs, nomadic Semites who devised the ingenious numerals we use today, yet whose early history was recorded only by others. In 100 years they carried their language and Islam religion to countries from Western India to Morocco and Southern Spain. In the process they spread the classic knowledge, architecture, art and foods of many ancient cultures wide and far.

This remarkable period was triggered by an obscure Arab born in Mecca in 570 A.D. who believed in the one just, merciful God of his Hebrew ancestors, and in the teachings of the Prophets. He became known as Mohammed (messenger) and wrote his own revelations from God in the Koran (the reading) to found the religion of Islam (submission). Followers became known as Moslems (those who submit to God), not "Mohammedens." In 622 he was forced to flee to Medina, and it is this date upon which the Arab calendar is based. In 630 he returned to Mecca, destroyed the idols, and turned the heathen temple into a mosque. Upon Mohammed's death in 632, Abu Bakr was elected caliph and became the first Moslem religious and political ruler. The *jihad* (holy war) that followed is unparalleled in history. Religious conversion was accompanied by political control, expansion of the arts and sciences, and increased trade. Like Christianity, Islam now embraces many ethnic groups, denominations and sects.

The Koran, like the Bible, is the basis for a number of taboos regarding food and drink. Strict Moslems abstain from alcohol, so I have omitted wines and liqueurs from many recipes where they can add delicate flavor. Indeed, many of my Middle Eastern friends highly recommend their use. It is interesting to note that coffee as it became popular in Middle East countries was given the Arab name for wine—*kahwah*. This "stygian lake, black, thick, bitter," as one early European visitor put it, became known as the "wine of Islam," though its name was changed to *kihwah* to distinguish it from wine. No one seems to know how this strange brew, apparently originating in Ethiopia, gained a foothold in Aden, then Mecca, Cairo, Damascus, Aleppo and Constantinople, but the South Yemen seaport of Mocha held a monopoly for 50 years before the Dutch in Java started growing it for export in 1720.

The religious taboo on pigs as a source of food is recognized as more than protection against supernatural reprisal. While it is usually attributed to early Hebrew knowledge of how quickly pork spoils in a hot climate, records indicate pork was acceptable at least until 1800 B.C. There are some who feel it was the nomads who imposed their will on others. They simply had no use for the pig. It had no stamina for traveling like the cow, sheep, goat or camel. It was cantankerous, ornery and impossible to herd and milk.

10

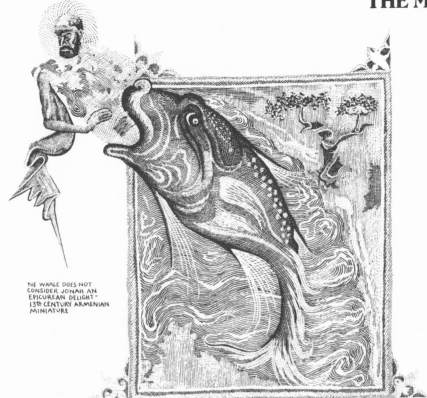

THE WHALE DOES NOT
CONSIDER JONAH AN
EPICUREAN DELIGHT—
13ᵗʰ CENTURY ARMENIAN
MINIATURE

Fasting plays a part in most religions. It was important to keep the whimsical early gods friendly by fasting in their honor (and at the same time stretch out meager food supplies). Egyptians coupled fasting's religious aspects with a preoccupation with their alimentary canals, supposedly the source of most illness, and would precede it by purges of figs. Fasting can be a supplication for pardon, a sign of mourning and sorrow, a way of attaining spiritual joy by transcending the physical. Jews have their Yom Kipper, Christians their Lent and Moslems their ninth month, Ramadan, a time for daily fasting from sunrise to sunset. Then, happily, great feasts and celebrations come along, joyous occasions with camaraderie and heaping platters of special foods. The heart, the soul and the body are reborn.

Sometimes I feel the people of the Middle East for centuries have been atoning for the excesses of their ancestors, for the forests denuded, the fields worn out by overuse, the cruelty of conquerors to the conquered, the pillaging and destruction of cities. It is my fervent hope that with their rather recent independence, important mineral wealth, and determination to rebuild cities, communities and irrigation systems, they will find more joyous times ahead with fellowship and feasting.

Now let's look at each major cuisine and its setting in more detail. Let's taste the foods and imagine ourselves as invited visitors at the tables of the Middle East. *Ahlen wah sahlen:* "The door is open—welcome."

NAZARENE GIRL REAPING GRAIN WITH SICKLE

ISRAEL

THE NEW Israeli nation founded in 1948 is a monument to the courage of a race eons old. It is gradually again becoming the promised land of milk and honey as it was in the time of Abraham 4000 years ago. Refugee descendants of the simple shepherd tribes, who migrated from Mesopotamia in 1900 B.C., adopted the Canaanite culture and united under King David to form a great kingdom 900 years later, are reassembling after centuries of scattering and persecution to carry on their ancient Hebrew language, religion and traditions.

Israel's thoughts dwell on the future as well as on the past, however. Scholars are modernizing the language for speech, scholarship and science. The best features from many lands of exile are being incorporated into industry, agriculture, architecture, arts and sciences. New styles of living, of building, of working and of food and clothing are constantly erupting from this unique melting pot. The Israelis—literally, wrestlers with God (after Jacob who wrestled an angel and became known as Israel)—are wrestling with Nature and winning. Overcoming hardship with perserverance and faith in God is built into the history of a people who were enslaved by Egyptians in 1300 B.C. and again by Babylonians in 570 B.C., who were conquered and scattered by Assyrians in 720 B.C. (the "ten lost tribes") and later by the Romans in 70 A.D. when Jerusalem and its temple (only the "Wailing Wall" remains) were destroyed. The durability of their culture and religion in the face of persecution during wanderings around the globe is legendary.

Jewish people consider food a precious gift from God. Their cookbooks are the history of 4000 years of happiness and sorrow. For example, the *latke* (pancake) was fed to the soldiers of Judah Maccabee battling Assyrian warriors. Sweets at a wedding portend a sweet life together, at Rosh Hashonah (New Year), a sweet year ahead. Each Sabbath eve, delightful aromas of simmering soup, golden chicken, baking *challah,* or other special dishes fill the air, for religious tradition permits only feasting, not working or cooking on the morrow.

13

ISRAEL

The long-neglected land is again being made productive by fierce determination. Swamps are being drained, depleted soil fertilized, scarce water distributed by pipes and ditches and new crops are being tried. New social patterns are also being developed, based on groups somewhat like the ancient tribes. The *moshavot* are villages of individual family-owned farms with co-operative purchasing and marketing. In the more revolutionary *kibbutzim* (gatherings), communal living is succeeding as never before. Every able-bodied person works—including the very young, the old and the disabled—and shares equally the fruits of labor. There is no need for money. Here hands link to each other in unparalleled unity to bring forth abundance from the slumbering earth in a veritable rhapsody of the spirit of one for all and all for one.

Religion reaches all phases of food for the Jewish people—into the packing house, in the kitchen and at the table. Long ago the *Talmud* prescribed in detail the role of various foods for the Sabbath, special feasts and fasts, and the dietary laws of *kashruth* (fitness). The origin of these laws is variously explained as hygienic, or due to practical problems such as difficulty in herding pigs, or necessary for spiritual discipline, or as a means of retaining Jewish identity. Blood was not to be eaten because it was the life of flesh. The required separation of milk and meat is thought to have originated from ancient idolatrous rites involving kid cooked in its mother's milk.

The presiding deity in the heart of the household, the kitchen, is the wife-mother-cook, who provides her menfolk and children with pleasures for the palate and strength to meet adversity. She must learn the intricate rules of obtaining kosher meats from which the blood and diseased parts have been properly removed; of separating milk and meat in cooking (including utensils) and at meals; of which foods are forbidden, such as seafoods without scales and fins (eels, oysters, etc.), pork and cheese containing the animal tissue "rennet" (stomach lining used to curdle milk); of which foods are *parere,* or neutral, and can be served with either milk or meat separately (fish, unfertilized eggs, vegetables, insect-free fruit).

Early Israelites added the breads, grains, lentils, beans, olives, vegetables and wine of the Canaanites to the milk and meat of sheep and goats, potherbs for cooking and green herbs raw, and occasional fruits of their previous nomadic life. Such foods still predominate, enriched by innumerable delicacies from lands of exile and new fruits and vegetables of which their ancestors never dreamed.

To the oppressed, physically conquered yet spiritually free, sharing is a way of life. The Jewish people are generous and hospitable beyond the ordinary. Their *shalom aleichem* (peace to you) is said with special warmth to the stranger. Yet no Jew, no matter what his station, can be happier than sharing with his own people the feasts and festivals of the ages and the traditional foods that along with religion have sustained him and made him strong.

CHICKEN LIVER PÂTÉ

Sauté until livers are tender in:
1/2 cup rendered chicken fat
2 pounds chicken livers, cut up
2 medium onions, sliced
1 bay leaf
1 garlic clove, chopped
1/2 teaspoon salt
1/4 teaspoon pepper
Do not overcook. Cool slightly and on fine blade of grinder, grind twice with:
2 hard-cooked eggs, chopped
Blend in:
1/2 cup brandy
Adjust seasonings to taste with salt and pepper. Mound on large serving platter or wooden plank. Flank with:
stuffed hard-cooked eggs
parsley sprigs
Top with:
grated hard-cooked egg yolk
Serve with an assortment of breads such as rye, dark rye, pumpernickel and bland crackers.
Makes approximately 40 individual appetizer servings

EGGS STUFFED WITH CHICKEN LIVER PÂTÉ

Use chicken liver pâté to mix with hard-cooked egg yolks to make stuffed eggs. Garnish each with a caper.

COSTA'S CHICKEN LIVER PÂTÉ IN PHYLLO

Chill chicken liver pâté (preceding recipe). Place between 2 sheets of wax paper and gradually press and shape into a rectangle approximately 8x12 inches and 1/2 inch thick. Chill and unwrap onto board. Place lengthwise in a row in center of rectangle:
5 small hard-cooked eggs

Roll and pat pâté mixture into a log about 8 inches long, encasing eggs completely. Have ready:
14 phyllo sheets (see Basics)
sweet butter
Butter sheets, stack as directed and place pâté roll on short end of phyllo. Fold over once, turn in edges and roll like jelly roll. Place seam side down on buttered baking sheet and brush liberally with:
melted sweet butter
Bake in 350° oven 15 minutes; lower heat to 300° and continue baking, basting several times with melted sweet butter, approximately 20 minutes or until phyllo is golden. If top browns too fast, cover loosely with foil. Remove to serving platter or board and let cool slightly. Slice diagonally into 3/4-inch slices and serve with assorted breads and/or unsalted crackers.
Makes approximately 12 slices

ISRAEL

ISRAELI PICKLED HERRING

In water to cover soak overnight:
2 salted herrings
Fillet and bone herrings, cut into pieces 2 inches square and set aside. Slice thinly and set aside:
2 large onions
Bring to boil, remove from heat and cool slightly:
1 cup white vinegar
1/4 cup water
1 tablespoon sugar
4 peppercorns
1 tablespoon pickling spices
3 bay leaves
1 tablespoon freshly squeezed lemon juice
Pack herring and onions alternately in hot sterilized 1-pint wide-mouth jar. Place on top of each onion layer 1 tablespoon of the vinegar mixture. Add rest of liquid to fill jar up to 1 inch. Drizzle with:
1 tablespoon olive oil (optional)
Seal and refrigerate 1 week or longer. Serve with sour cream.
Makes 1 pint

EGGPLANT SALAD

Cook in 400° oven until charred on outside and soft on inside:
1 large eggplant
Cool, remove skin and coarsely chop eggplant. Place in colander to drain moisture. Mash or purée in blender. Stir in:
1/4 cup mayonnaise
2 hard-cooked eggs, finely chopped
1/2 cup finely chopped pickles
1/4 cup each minced parsley and onion
2 garlic cloves, finely minced
3 tablespoons olive oil
2 tablespoons lemon or lime juice
salt and pepper to taste
Place in oiled mold and chill thoroughly. Unmold on platter and decorate with:
thin strips of green pepper
Surround with:
lemon wedges
quartered ripe tomatoes
thinly sliced onion rings
Serve with assorted breads such as pumpernickel, light or dark rye, toast triangles.
Serves 4 to 6

SCRIBE AND TORAH

I am given to understand that there is a considerable ceremony surrounding the handling of the Torah. This sequence is not altogether clear to me, but I think it involves prayer, ablution and special writing tools. There are also rules of conduct governing interruption and resumption of the work, as well as the occurrence of error in the transcribing of the manuscript.

SCRIBE REPAIRING TORAH

ISRAEL

CUCUMBER SOUR CREAM MOLD

Slice thinly on slicing attachment of grater:
1-1/2 large peeled cucumbers
Reserve unpeeled half for garnish. Sprinkle sliced cucumbers liberally with:
salt
Let stand in colander to drain 30 minutes. Rinse and dry on paper toweling. Set aside.
Soften in:
1/3 cup water
1 envelope unflavored gelatin
Dissolve over hot water, cool and combine with:
1 pint sour cream, whipped
1/4 cup lemon juice
1 teaspoon lemon extract
1 tablespoon sugar
1 teaspoon grated lemon peel
2 tablespoons minced mint
1/2 teaspoon salt
**1/4 teaspoon freshly ground
   black pepper**
Adjust seasonings to taste. In round 4- to 6-cup mold arrange about one-third of the sliced cucumbers in concentric pattern. Carefully pour over them half of the sour cream mixture.

Arrange remaining slices on top and cover with remaining sour cream. Cover and chill 6 hours or until set. Score remaining cucumber half with fork and slice thinly by hand. Turn mold out onto chilled serving plate and surround in alternate overlapping pattern with:
reserved unpeeled cucumber slices
lemon slices
Form a border with:
parsley sprigs
Serves 6 to 8

ISRAELI SALAD

The kibbutzim is the creator of a salad now adopted by bistros from Paris to America—an array of vegetables, cleaned and left whole, arranged artistically in a large wooden bowl or on a tray or platter, chilled and served with a variety of dressings. Guests choose at will from your gourmet canvas and create their own salad.

Wash, dry and chill any or all of the following:
wedges of lettuce and cabbage
green and red pepper rings
whole tomatoes
radishes
celery stalks
green onion stalks
cucumbers
whole carrots
kohlrabi
Arrange in wooden bowl or on serving platter. Surround with bowls of:
sliced cooked beets
hard-cooked eggs
lemon wedges
chopped gherkins
anchovy fillets
green and black olives
chopped pickled herring
herb sprigs in season
Give each guest a spoon and a small bowl in which to mix dressings. For making dressings, provide:
**cruets of olive oil, garlic olive
   oil and vinegar**
bowls of sour cream and yoghurt
prepared mustard
peppermill
coarse salt
paprika
Serve with:
pita (page 132)

AVOCADO SOUP

In heavy saucepan over low heat melt:

4 tablespoons butter

Add and cook slowly 5 minutes:

5 1/2-inch slices ginger root

Stir in:

1/4 cup flour

Cook and stir 3 minutes and gradually add:

1-1/2 cups milk
1/2 to 1 teaspoon grated fresh lemon peel

Cook over low heat, stirring often, 10 minutes until sauce is smooth and thick. It will take on flavor of the ginger root. Discard ginger root and remove from heat. Cool slightly. In blender purée:

2 large avocados
1/2 cup milk
1/2 teaspoon salt

Blend puréed avocados into sauce and add:

1/2 to 1 cup heavy cream

Chill thoroughly and adjust with salt. Serve in chilled bowls with garnish of:

avocado balls rubbed with lemon juice

Serves 6

THE SHRINE OF THE BOOK AT THE ISRAEL MUSEUM, JERUSALEM, IN WHICH ARE HOUSED THE DEAD SEA SCROLLS

ISRAEL

COLD FRUIT SOUP

Starting a meal with a cold fruit soup is a refreshing custom in Israel.

Combine and cook 20 minutes or until fruits are tender:

1 cup pitted sour red cherries, halved
1 cup sliced peaches
1 cup chopped pitted plums
1 cup grated green apple
1 cup sugar
6 cups water
1 teaspoon lemon juice
1 2-inch stick cinnamon
4 whole cloves
1/4 teaspoon salt

Discard cinnamon stick and cloves and force through sieve or food mill. Reheat with:

1-1/2 tablespoons cornstarch, dissolved in
3 tablespoons water

Cook and stir until slightly thickened, cool and add:

1 cup half-and-half
3 tablespoons Sabra*

Chill thoroughly, adjust with more Sabra and/or lemon juice. Serve in chilled compote glasses with:

dollop of sour cream topped with a maraschino cherry

Serves 6

*Liqueur imported from Israel made with oranges from Jaffa and a touch of chocolate—a superb flavor. Available in Middle Eastern stores. Or substitute any fruit liqueur.

2ND CENTURY PALESTINIAN GLASS WINE VESSEL

MATZO BALLS
IN CHICKEN SOUP

In Israel chicken soup is served with a wide variety of accompaniments. Matzo balls are the classic favorite. Their preparation requires a light hand.

Blend well:
2 eggs, beaten
2 tablespoons rendered chicken fat, softened
Add and stir in, mixing well:
1 teaspoon salt
1/2 cup matzo meal
Blend in:
additional 2 tablespoons rendered chicken fat, softened
Cover and refrigerate at least 1 hour. Dampen hands with water and form mixture into balls about the size of a small egg, smoothing gently. Bring to boil:
2 cups each chicken stock and water or
4 cups lightly salted water
3 tablespoons rendered chicken fat

Lower heat to *slow* boil; drop balls in, cover and cook 20 to 25 minutes. Heat:
2 quarts chicken stock
Adjust seasonings and remove matzo balls with slotted spoon to the stock. Bring just to boil and serve immediately.
Makes approximately 10 balls (they double in size)

SOPHIE'S LOX OMELET

The classic breakfast or brunch is not complete without lox, bagels and cream cheese served in a variety of ways. Omelets with chicken livers, lox with scrambled eggs, onions, herring— all belong on the table.
This version is a definite must, not only for taste but for eye appeal.

Brown in:
2 tablespoons butter
1 cup chopped onions
Add, simmer 3 minutes and set aside:
2 cups minced lox
Beat together:
5 eggs
2 teaspoons half-and-half

Heat a heavy skillet or omelet pan and swirl in:
1 tablespoon butter
Add:
beaten eggs
Shake pan gently while cooking so egg forms an omelet and covers bottom of pan. When bottom is set but eggs are still moist on top, quickly place in center strip:
half the reserved onions and lox
Top with:
3 tablespoons sour cream
Tip pan slightly and with spatula fold omelet edges toward center. Heat 2 minutes and gently turn out onto heated serving platter. Repeat process with:
5 more eggs and 2 teaspoons half-and-half
Turn out second omelet alongside first and garnish with:
strips of lox
Flank one side of platter with:
1/2 pint sour cream
Serve immediately with:
toasted bagels
cream cheese
Serves 6

THE PERSONAL RING SEAL OF THE RAMBAN, 1267

THE PERSONAL RING SEAL OF THE RAMBAN, 1267

The Ramban, one of the greatest Jewish scholars in Spain of 700 years ago, engaged in a public dispute in Barcelona at the order of King Jaime the First. He won, and in 1265 he was accused of blasphemy for the publication of his words in that debate.
In 1267, he moved to the Holy Land and reorganized the Jewish community in Jerusalem. He died in Acre three years later. The seal, less than an inch in diameter, was found early in 1972 near Tel-Kaisun, five miles south of Acre.

LEEK PATTIES

Leeks are the most ignored vegetable in American cookery. This noble plant has a heritage in Middle Eastern cooking as far back as the early Egyptians who regarded them highly. It is unfortunate we do not have more recipes for leeks, rather than relegating them almost exclusively to the soup pot.

Simmer until tender in water to cover:
1 bunch leeks (approximately 6), white part only
Chop leeks finely and combine with:
2 eggs, beaten
1 cup matzo meal
1 tablespoon cooking oil
1/2 teaspoon salt
1/4 teaspoon freshly ground black pepper
Adjust seasonings, blend well, chill and form into patties.
Brown patties on both sides in:
vegetable oil
Serve hot as accompaniment to meat, fish or fowl.
Serves 4

SWEET POTATO AND CARROT TZIMMES

Boil separately until tender:
3 large sweet potatoes or yams
6 large carrots
Mash thoroughly and set aside.
Sauté until tender in:
6 tablespoons butter
1 large onion, minced
Remove onion from heat, add and blend well:
reserved sweet potatoes and carrots
3/4 cup raisins soaked in Sabra* to cover
1/4 cup toasted slivered blanched almonds
3 tablespoons honey
1 tablespoon grated fresh orange rind
1 teaspoon grated lemon rind
salt and pepper to taste
Place in well-buttered casserole and bake in 375° oven 20 minutes. Sprinkle with:
minced parsley
Serve from casserole.
Serves 6
*Liqueur imported from Israel made with oranges from Jaffa and a touch of chocolate. Available in Middle Eastern stores.

ISRAEL

SECOND CENTURY B.C. BRONZE OIL LAMP FROM
AVDAT IN THE NEGEV DESERT

FELAFEL
(Garbanzo Bean Croquettes)

Soak in hot water to cover
20 minutes:
1/4 cup fine bulghur
Combine bulghur with:
**2 cups cooked garbanzo beans
   (see Basics), mashed**
2 garlic cloves, finely minced
3 tablespoons bread crumbs
1 egg, beaten
1/2 teaspoon each salt and cumin
**1/4 teaspoon each black pepper,
   turmeric and coriander**
1 tablespoon minced parsley
1/8 teaspoon cayenne pepper
Adjust seasonings and chill. Shape
into 12 to 16 balls, roll in flour
and fry in deep fat until golden.

Drain croquettes on paper toweling. Cut a pocket in:
**12 to 16 pita bread discs
   (page 132)**
Place a croquette in each
pocket and fill with a spoonful of:
relish (following)
**tahini dressing made with cayenne
   pepper to taste (see Basics)**
Serves 6 to 8

RELISH FOR FELAFEL

Combine:
**2 ripe tomatoes, peeled and
   finely minced**
1 green pepper, finely minced
1/2 cup chopped parsley
**1 cucumber, peeled and finely
   minced**
**salt, black pepper and cayenne
   pepper to taste**

BEEF IN SAUERKRAUT SAUCE

Rinse once in cold water,
drain and set aside:
1 32-ounce jar sauerkraut
Brown on all sides in:
3 tablespoons rendered beef fat
1 3- to 4-pound beef brisket (or any economy-size cut of beef)
Remove promptly and set aside.
In a separate skillet gently brown
until transparent in:
1 tablespoon rendered beef fat
2 large onions, thinly sliced
Add and mix well:
reserved sauerkraut
2 large apples, grated
2 medium potatoes, grated
1 tablespoon brown sugar
2 bay leaves, crumbled
1/2 teaspoon each salt and caraway seeds
1/4 teaspoon freshly ground black pepper
Place half of mixture in bottom
of heavy saucepan or Dutch oven.
Lay brisket on top and cover
with remaining sauerkraut
mixture.

Pour in:
1 cup beef broth or water
1 cup dry white wine (optional; if not using, add water or broth)
Cover and simmer over low fire,
stirring and basting frequently,
2 hours or until meat is tender.
Add additional water or broth
during cooking if needed. Place
meat on a large heated platter,
slice and surround with sauce.
Serves 4 to 6

APPLES STUFFED WITH CURRIED CHICKEN

This is a superb recipe that may
be served as a complete meal.
Smaller apples may also be
stuffed and used to garnish your
holiday menus.

Wash and dry:
8 large cooking apples
Core and scoop out pulp, leaving
a shell about 1/2 inch thick.
Reserve pulp for apple soup or
apple strudel. Set apple shells
aside.
Soak and set aside:
1/2 cup raisins in
brandy to cover

In saucepan melt:
2 tablespoons margarine
Sprinkle with:
2 tablespoons flour
Cook and stir 3 minutes and
gradually add:
1 cup rich chicken broth
Cook and stir until thickened
and blend in:
2 chicken breasts, boiled, skinned, boned and chopped
4 cups steamed rice (see Basics, curry variation)
1/2 cup chopped almonds or walnuts
reserved raisins, drained
2 tablespoons brown sugar
1/2 teaspoon cinnamon
1/4 teaspoon each powdered cloves and ginger
Adjust seasonings to taste and
stuff apples. Place remaining
rice mixture in mold, cover and
place in pan of water in oven.
Place apples in buttered baking
dish, cover and bake apples and
rice mold in 300° oven 40 minutes or until apples are tender.
Unmold rice on center of heated
platter. Surround with apples
and over all sprinkle:
2 cups cooked peas
Serves 8

ISRAEL

TONGUE IN BRANDIED FRUIT SAUCE

In large heavy kettle place:
1 fresh beef tongue (4 to 5 pounds)
2 onions, coarsely chopped
1 celery rib and leaves, coarsely chopped
2 garlic cloves
3 bay leaves
1 lemon, sliced
4 parsley sprigs
1 tablespoon salt
10 peppercorns, lightly crushed
water to cover
Bring to gentle boil, cover and simmer 2-1/2 to 3 hours or until tongue is tender. Meanwhile combine and let stand 1 hour:
12 pitted prunes
12 dried figs
1 cup each raisins and blanched almonds
Sabra* to cover
Remove tongue, strain broth and reserve. Skin and trim tongue and return to broth. Add fruits and Sabra and:
3 tablespoons brown sugar
1 teaspoon each cinnamon and allspice
1 cup Mandorcrema**

Bring back to boil, cover and simmer 20 minutes or until fruits are tender. Cool with lid tilted, cover and refrigerate overnight. Remove 6 prunes and 6 figs and stuff each with:
chopped blanched almonds
Set aside. Return kettle to heat and add:
2 tablespoons cornstarch, dissolved in
1/2 cup Mandorcrema
Cook and stir until thickened. Remove tongue, slice thinly and arrange on heated platter. Pour sauce over and garnish with:
reserved stuffed prunes and figs
Serve with extra sauce.
Serves 8
 *Liqueur imported from Israel made with oranges and a touch of chocolate. Available in Middle Eastern stores.
**Almond cream marsala available in Middle Eastern stores and liquor stores.

SHASHLIK WITH KASHA PILAF

Split and cut in half:
6 lamb kidneys
Cut into 1-inch cubes:
1-1/2 pounds baby beef liver
1 pound beef filet
1 small unpeeled eggplant
1 green pepper
1 large onion
Skewer meat and vegetables alternately, including:
cherry tomatoes
Set skewers in shallow pan and sprinkle with:
salt and freshly ground pepper to taste
Pour over and turn to coat well:
2 tablespoons each lemon juice and melted rendered chicken fat
Place under broiler or over coals, and basting and turning often, cook 15 to 20 minutes. Serve on a bed of kasha pilaf (following) and garnish with:
parsley sprigs
lemon wedges
Serves 4

KASHA PILAF

In heavy skillet gently brown:
2 cups whole kasha (buckwheat groats)
Add and stir until grains are separated:
1 egg, lightly beaten
In separate skillet brown in:
6 tablespoons rendered goose or chicken fat
1 onion, chopped
Add to kasha with:
4 cups hot chicken broth
Stir well, cover and simmer about 25 minutes. Kasha should be tender and broth and fat absorbed. Toss with fork to keep grains separated, adding:
4 tablespoons butter, softened
Adjust seasonings with salt and pepper to taste. Mound on large heated serving platter.

KASHA-STUFFED CHICKEN

"A man can live without spices, but not without wheat."
Talmud

Prepare and set aside:
1-1/2 recipes kasha pilaf (preceding)
Prepare for roasting:
1 5- to 6-pound chicken
Boil in water until tender:
giblets from chicken
Remove from water, mince and set aside.
Boil until prunes are tender and set aside:
1-1/2 cups dried pitted prunes
3 tablespoons sugar
water to just cover
Sauté until tender in:
3 tablespoons rendered goose or chicken fat
2 onions, minced
3 celery stalks, minced
3 tablespoons minced parsley
minced cooked giblets
1/2 teaspoon salt
1/4 teaspoon pepper
Add and blend well:
reserved kasha pilaf
reserved prunes, drained and minced (reserve juice)
1/4 cup Sabra*
1/2 teaspoon paprika

Adjust with salt and pepper to taste and stuff chicken with half the kasha mixture. Place in roasting pan and roast in 450° oven 15 minutes. Lower heat to 350° and continue roasting 1 hour or until tender, basting often with:
pan juices
1/4 cup reserved prune juice
Pack into 6 1/2-cup buttered molds:
remaining kasha pilaf mixture
Last 30 minutes of roasting, place molds in pan of hot water and bake in oven with chicken. Remove chicken from oven, scoop out stuffing and set aside. Pour over chicken and return to oven to keep warm:
2 tablespoons Sabra
Toss into stuffing:
2 cups hot cooked fine noodles
(This is called kasha varnitchkes.) Place in heated serving bowl. Remove chicken to heated platter and turn out kasha molds around chicken. Garnish with:
cherry tomatoes
Serve pan juices separately.
Serves 6 to 8
*Liqueur imported from Israel made with oranges from Jaffa.

ISRAEL

GOOSE WITH MATZO STUFFING

Render fat from:
1 8- to 10-pound goose
Add enough rendered chicken fat to make 1/2 cup and set aside. Wash and pat dry the goose and rub inside and out with mixture of:
3 tablespoons each rendered goose fat and freshly grated orange rind
juice of 1 large lemon
1 teaspoon salt
1/2 teaspoon pepper

Sauté until onions are transparent in:
remaining goose fat
2 onions, finely chopped
1/2 cup chopped celery and leaves
chopped goose liver and gizzard
1/4 cup minced parsley
2 apples, grated
2 teaspoons paprika
Remove from heat and blend in:
1 cup chopped walnuts
1-1/2 to 2 cups chopped prunes which have been softened in water and drained
2 cups matzo meal
1 cup chicken stock
1/2 cup fresh orange juice
2 eggs, beaten

Toss ingredients well and stuff into goose cavity. Skewer cavity and lace. Place goose on rack in baking pan. Bake in 325° oven approximately 3-1/2 hours, basting frequently and removing fat from top of juices. Add water to roasting pan if needed. Last 1/2 hour of cooking baste with mixture of:
1/2 cup brandy
1 tablespoon honey
1 teaspoon grated orange rind
Remove to heated platter and to pan add:
2 tablespoons orange preserves
1/2 cup fruit wine
Heat and pour half the juices over goose. Garnish with:
orange slices
Serve with extra pan juices.

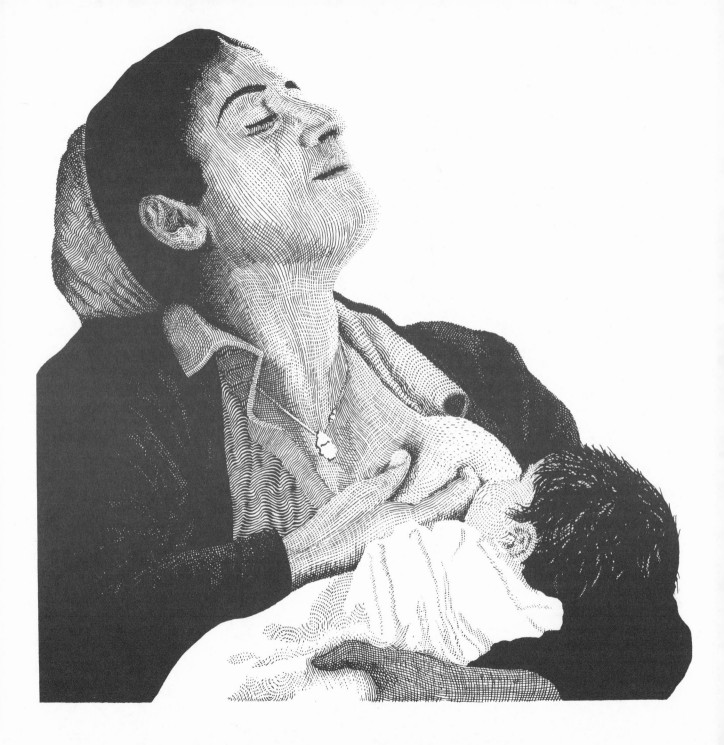

ISRAEL

A STAR OF DAVID STYLED AFTER THE ISRAELI FLAG

CHOLLET

"He who prepares before the Sabbath can eat on the Sabbath."
  Jonathan ben Eleazar

On a Sabbath, the aromas tantalize and bring the hearth close to a Jew, no matter where he has roamed or what gastronomical delights he has tasted! This above all is home. The freshly baked challah, the soup of all soups set before him and now the simple but eternal chollet—and the day has ended well. Chollet is also called chulent, cholent, chollent and shalet.

In water to cover soak overnight:
3 cups dried lima beans
Drain and set aside.
In Dutch oven, brown on all sides in:
2 tablespoons rendered chicken fat
1 5-pound brisket of beef
1/4 cup chopped onion
1 garlic clove, minced (optional)

Season while browning with:
1-1/2 teaspoons salt
1/2 teaspoon freshly ground
   black pepper
1/4 teaspoon each paprika,
   cinnamon and powdered ginger
Add:
reserved lima beans
1 cup pearl barley
16 small peeled potatoes
4 carrots
2 turnips
2 parsley roots (optional)
2 onions, chopped
Sprinkle all with:
2 tablespoons flour
1 tablespoon paprika
Add to cover 1 inch above
ingredients:
boiling water
Cover tightly and bake in 350°
oven 3 to 4 hours or until meat
is tender. Slice meat and arrange
on heated serving platter. Surround with beans, barley and
vegetables. Sprinkle with:
1/2 cup minced parsley
Serve with pan juices on the side.
Serves 8 to 10

CHALLAH

The challah is the traditional
Sabbath and holiday bread.
The versions and shape of the
challah vary. I prefer the eight
braid which is the classic work
of art and have simplified the
method of preparing it here.

In small shallow bowl dissolve in:
1/2 cup lukewarm water
1 cake yeast
Melt in:
1/2 cup warm milk
1/2 pound sweet butter
2 teaspoons sugar
Mix in:
6 eggs, beaten
Add to dissolved yeast.
In large mixing bowl sift:
4 cups flour
1 teaspoon salt
Make a hollow in center of flour
and pour in egg mixture. Mix
with wooden spoon or hands
to blend ingredients thoroughly,
adding more flour if needed.
Knead until smooth. Place dough

on floured board and knead
until firm, smooth and no longer
sticky, adding more flour if
needed. Shape into ball and
place in oiled bowl. Brush with
salad oil, cover with tea towel
and let rise in warm place about
2 hours or until double in bulk.
Punch dough down and knead
briefly. Set aside to rest 10 minutes. Divide into 8 equal pieces.
On lightly floured board roll
each piece into a rope about 20
inches long. Braid three ropes
in standard braid and place on
buttered baking pan. Braid 3
more ropes and place alongside
first braid, about 1-1/2 inches
away. Braid remaining 2 ropes
and place in the center on top
of braided sections.
Brush lightly with:
beaten egg yolk
Sprinkle generously with:
poppy seeds
Cover with tea towel and let rise
another hour. Bake in 375° oven
approximately 1 hour.

ISRAEL

MANDELBROT

This is my sister-in-law Sophie's version of almond bread, which is traditionally baked in round cake pans layer upon layer. This is a simplified and delicious cake.

Combine and set aside:
1/2 cup chopped blanched almonds
2 tablespoons each sugar
   and cinnamon
In mixing bowl, sift:
2 cups white flour
1/4 teaspoon salt
Combine and beat well:
6 eggs
1 cup sugar
Combine well into flour. Butter an angel-food cake pan and pour in 1/4 of the batter. Sprinkle with 1/4 of the nut mixture.

Repeat to make 4 layers. Bake in 350° oven approximately 45 minutes. Remove and cool slightly. Turn onto cutting board and slice 1/4 inch thick. Place slices on lightly buttered cookie sheet and brown lightly in 425° oven.
Makes approximately 25 to 30 slices

MANDELBROT ROLL

This almond roll is sure to be a favorite. The choice of fillings is optional but all guaranteed to be delicious.

In mixing bowl sift:
2 cups flour
2 teaspoons baking powder
Make a well in center and pour in:
4 eggs, beaten with
1 cup sugar
2 tablespoons salad oil
Mix well and turn out onto floured board. Knead well, using oil as needed to coat hands.

Dough should be smooth. Dusting with sifted flour, roll into a rectangle approximately 12x15 inches. Brush lavishly with:
melted butter
Spread over rectangle a generous layer of:
imported Israeli orange preserves*
Over layer of preserves sprinkle:
3/4 cup sultanas
1 tablespoon freshly grated orange rind
1/2 cup chopped blanched almonds
Roll as a jelly roll and seal ends. Place on buttered cookie sheet seam side down and bake in 350° oven 35 to 40 minutes until gently browned. Cool, place on serving plate and dust generously with:
sifted powdered sugar
*Imported lemon marmalade and/or ginger and/or apricot preserves may be substituted.

CARROT CAKE

Beat until smooth and lemon-colored:
9 egg yolks
Gradually beat in until thick:
1-1/2 cups fine sugar
Stir in:
1-1/2 cups puréed cooked carrots
2-1/2 cups ground almonds (do not grind in blender; use a nut grinder or the almonds will release their oil)
1 tablespoon grated orange rind
1 teaspoon grated lemon rind
1 tablespoon Sabra*
1/2 teaspoon cinnamon
Whip until stiff:
9 egg whites (room temperature)
Gradually fold egg whites into carrot mixture until blended. Build up sides of a 9-inch springform cake pan with heavy aluminum foil. Butter pan and foil well and pour in cake mixture. Bake in 325° oven 50 to 60 minutes. Do not open oven door first 40 minutes. Cool on rack and remove from pan.
*Liqueur imported from Israel made with oranges from Jaffa and a touch of chocolate. Available in Middle Eastern stores.

PRUNE AND ORANGE DESSERT MOLD

Use a large, deep 8-cup mold.
For first layer soften in:
3 tablespoons cold water
1 tablespoon lemon juice
1 envelope gelatin
Heat and blend:
1/2 cup prune juice
2 teaspoons firmly packed dark brown sugar
Add and dissolve:
softened gelatin
Remove from heat and add:
1/2 teaspoon grated orange rind
1 tablespoon brandy
3 tablespoons finely chopped walnuts
1/8 teaspoon salt
Cool and fold in:
2/3 cup heavy cream, whipped
Refrigerate until cold and pour into mold that has been rinsed in cold water. Refrigerate.

For second layer, soften in:
1/2 cup fruit juice
2 envelopes gelatin
Heat and add to dissolve:
3 cups fruit juice
softened gelatin
2 tablespoons each imported quince preserves and imported orange preserves
1/4 cup Sabra*
Remove from heat and cool slightly. Pour a small layer of fruit gelatin on jelled prune mixture (should be almost solid). Refrigerate until set and arrange on top:
small orange sections
halved grapes
Pour in another layer of fruit gelatin and refrigerate until set. Repeat process until mold is filled. Cover with saran and chill 6 hours or until set. Unmold on chilled serving plate and decorate with mixture of:
2/3 cup heavy cream, whipped
2 tablespoons imported orange preserves (put in blender if using pastry tube to decorate)
*Liqueur imported from Israel made with oranges from Jaffa and a touch of chocolate. Available in Middle Eastern stores.

KURDISH GIRLS NEAR TAQ-I-BUSTAN

PERSIA

IN 1925 the Riza Shah decided the Persian people had been pawns of history long enough. It was time to shed the veils that hid women's beauty, to purge the language of Arab and Turkish words, to revitalize a nation that had been under the domination of vying Turks, British and Russians since 1787. The name chosen in 1935 for this nation reborn, striving to solve ancient problems with a modern approach, was "Iran," after Indo-European speaking Aryans from the Asian steppes who first settled here in 2000 B.C. But its culture and people retained the name "Persian" from Persis in the south, which had been united with Media in the north 2500 years ago by the mighty Cyrus.

Under Cyrus, the Medes and Persians conquered Asia Minor, Assyria, Babylonia and Egypt. This empire peaked under Darius in the 400's B.C. with a strong government that ruled from India to Greece. Coins, roads and irrigation tunnels supplied the means for commerce and greater food production. Xerxes and Alexander halted the Persian expansion, but during the period 260 to 600 A.D. Persia defeated the Romans and ruled the Tigris-Euphrates valley, the birthplace of civilization now part of Iraq.

Arab caliphs (religious leaders) ruled Persia from 641 A.D. well into the 800's and quickly traded their meager fare for Persian banquets, their simple talk for poetry and erudite gastronomic conversations. Even princes wrote cookbooks. When the Moslem empire crumbled, Persia reverted to small kingdoms, which remained centers of art, literature and science. But the Turks in 1037 and Ghenghis Khan in 1221 destroyed not only the culture of Persia but also the irrigation systems. However, new levels of excellence were reached under the Safavid Dynasty (1590 to 1730), Persia's last period of glory until the nationalism of the 1950's, fueled by rich reserves of oil. It was in the early 1600's that Shah Abbas the Great achieved his *Xanada* (dream of beauty) in the high city of Isfahan (from "half the world") by building colorful domes, minarets and façades rivaling in beauty the deep turquoise of the sky.

Most of Iran is harsh desert, mountains, salt lakes and high plateaus. Little wonder its inhabitants tried to compensate by creating their own paradise on earth in riotous color of temples, gardens and

PERSIA

paintings. Even the common people have long participated by weaving rugs patterned after formal gardens. Over 100,000 families today produce carpets to spread beauty throughout the world, each family following its own traditional design. The British painter Sargent declared, "There is more art in a really great carpet than in any picture ever painted."

The pomp of old Persia is preserved, too, in a literature ranked among the richest of the world, filled with tall tales and dry wit and illustrated again and again by great artists. The classical poetic style of the 10th century is well known to readers of Omar Khayyam, but Persians treasure more highly the writings of Firdausi, their greatest poet. His *Shah-Nama* (book of kings) is a long, epic poem to the first legendary ruler who invented cooking.

Omar's idyllic diet of a loaf of bread, a jug of wine, and love may appeal to some, but most Persians would prefer a *chelo kebab* of basmati rice, marinated lamb, *mast* (yoghurt), raw egg and sumac along with the bread, and hot tea sipped through a cube of sugar might supplement the wine. Then, of course, they might like to add "eggs of the sun" (apricots), slices of a 9-inch orange or 100-pound melon, or a wedge of nourishing goat's milk cheese.

The poor man's cow, the goat, is believed to have originated in the rugged, dry land of Persia. Here its stamina and ability to subsist on sparse, widely scattered vegetation made it an ideal candidate for domestication by wandering humans with less durable digestive systems. The goat's milk, already homogenized, sweet and easier to digest, with more fat and protein than cow's milk, made poor butter, but fabulous cheeses. Even today, 10 percent of Iran's population consists of wandering tribes who herd their goats and sheep from high mountains in the summer to warmer coastal areas during the winter.

Ten centuries ago in this great land bridge connecting the Middle and the Far East, long-grain rice and tea from the Orient revolutionized Persian food and drink. Now, in its low, wetter areas Iran grows most of its own rice. The *ghavakhane* (literally "coffee house," but in reality a tea house) serves the national drink, a hot sweet tea. Persian cuisine is based on rice, with other foods as satellites. The rice is often spiced with Indian mango, herbs or saffron, and an egg or bits of mutton may be added to enhance it. The Persians' insatiable sweet tooths call for honey, glazed fruits or sherbets, or even a syrupy pomegranate sauce over chunks of mutton.

Then there are the popular pistachios and the delicious skewered sturgeon and caviar of the salty Caspian Sea, along whose coast one finds tropical jungles. One of the most ancient of fishes, dating back some say 300 million years, the sturgeon is found in temperate fresh and salt waters throughout the Northern Hemisphere. The great beluga variety of the Middle East sometimes weighs over a ton, furnishing delicious fresh or smoked fillets and steaks, and roe for caviar.

The visitor to even the poorest wandering tribe of modern Iran may be invited to share a special feast. Persians are said to be born with the art of hospitality, with 60 ways of saying yes. In a typical flower of speech they may emotionally avow, "You may walk on my eyes!"

TONGUE AND PINEAPPLE PÂTÉ

Bring to boil and simmer 40 minutes or until tender:
6 young lamb tongues
water to cover
2 whole cloves
1 garlic clove, mashed
1 bay leaf
1 teaspoon salt
6 peppercorns, lightly crushed
Remove tongues. Strain liquid and reserve for another use. Skin tongues, slice half of one of the tongues into julienne and set aside. Chop remaining tongues and combine with:
2 slices fresh pineapple, diced
2 hard-cooked eggs, chopped
1 teaspoon allspice
1/2 teaspoon salt
1/4 teaspoon freshly ground
    black pepper
2 tablespoons butter, softened
1/4 cup pomegranate syrup
    (or brandy)
1/2 cup bread crumbs

Using fine blade of grinder, grind twice. Adjust seasonings to taste and mold into a loaf on wooden plank or serving platter. Chill well. Decorate with:
reserved julienne tongue
hard-cooked egg slices
Surround with:
small pineapple wedges
Serve with sesame bread and sesame crackers.
Makes approximately 25 appetizer servings

BELLY DANCER AT THE *MOULIN ROUGE* CLUB IN TEHRAN

PERSIA

SHAH'S SALAD

Combine and cook until tongues
are tender:
4 lamb tongues
water to cover
Drain, skin and cube tongues.
Set aside. Slice in half lengthwise:
1 large Persian melon
Using a melon scooper, scoop out
small balls, keeping shells intact.
Reserve shells for filling and
some of the melon balls for
garnish.
Combine:
melon balls
lamb tongue cubes
Combine:
3 cups plain yoghurt, chilled
1 cup pineapple juice
1 bunch seedless grapes
1 teaspoon each almond extract
   and honey
1/2 cup chopped walnuts
Toss melon balls and tongue with
half of the dressing. Fill melon
halves and chill. Chill remaining
yoghurt dressing. Just before
serving, garnish melon halves
with:
reserved melon balls
Serve with yoghurt dressing.
Serves 6

BORANI
(Cold Spinach Salad)

Wash, cut out tough stems and
coarsely chop:
2 large bunches fresh spinach
Place in large saucepan with:
1 large onion, grated
Cover and steam 5 minutes.
Strain in colander. Place in
wooden bowl and add, mixing
well:
2 cups plain yoghurt, beaten
2 tablespoons olive oil
1 tablespoon lemon juice
1/2 teaspoon salt
1/4 teaspoon freshly ground
   black pepper
1 garlic clove, finely minced
   (optional)
1/2 cup toasted chopped walnuts
Adjust seasonings, chill and
just before serving sprinkle with:
1 tablespoon toasted
   sesame seeds
2 tablespoons minced fresh mint
Garnish with:
lemon wedges
Serve with:
extra yoghurt
Serves 4 to 6

CARPET OF MAGICK

*From "1001 Arabian Nights,"
and Douglas Fairbanks' great
silent motion picture, "The
Thief of Bagdad," this tale has
every element of storytelling
expertise. These three princes
contend for the hand of the
Shah's daughter. One is too old,
another is corpulent, and the
third downright evil. The Shah
tells them to travel to distant
lands and return only with the
most exotic of gifts. The prince
bearing the most unusual prize
will receive the hand of the
princess.*
*The portly fellow finds a carpet
which delivers him in a twinkling
anywhere in the world. The
elderly gent locates a magic apple
which cures all disease and recent
death, and the evil prince comes
upon a crystal ball in which can
be seen events occurring anywhere in the world. They meet,
and upon gazing into the orb
they behold the princess lying
ill, poisoned near unto death.
Leaping onto the carpet, they
are whisked back to the palace
where they save the life of the
princess with the magic apple.
This combination of events
renders the problem insoluable,
and the whole story is left
hanging in the air until the
intervention of Hollywood
script writers, who enable Douglas Fairbanks to get the girl in
the end, after hanging the evil-
doers by their thumbs.*

CARPET OF MAGICK OVER ISFAHAN

PERSIA

DRIED FRUIT SOUP

Soak overnight in water to cover:
1/2 cup red beans (available in
    health food stores or specialty
    shops)
Drain and set aside.
Brown well in:
3 tablespoons olive oil
1 pound boneless lamb, cut
    in cubes
2/3 cup minced onion
1/2 teaspoon salt
1/4 teaspoon black pepper
1/8 teaspoon each turmeric,
    cardamom and cumin
Stir in and bring to boil:
6 cups lamb or chicken stock
reserved red beans
1/2 cup lentils, well washed
1 large beet, peeled and cut
    in julienne
Lower heat, cover and cook
slowly 1 hour. Add:
1 cup mixed dried fruit such as
    apricots, prunes, pears,
    peaches, all chopped
water or lamb stock to bring
    back to same level

Bring back to boil, cover and
simmer 30 minutes. Add:
3 tablespoons lemon juice
more stock if too thick
Reheat and adjust seasonings.
Serve garnished with:
minced parsley
lemon wedges
Serves 4 to 6

AASH
(Soup)

Soak overnight in water to cover:
1 cup red beans (available in
    health food stores or specialty
    shops; kidney beans may be
    substituted)
Drain and add:
2-1/2 cups water
Cook until almost tender, adding
more water if needed. Set aside.
Brown in:
1/4 cup olive oil
2 large onions, chopped
Season while browning with:
1/2 teaspoon turmeric
1/4 teaspoon cayenne pepper

Add:
1 quart lamb stock
1-1/2 quarts chicken stock
2 cups each cooked garbanzo
    beans and lentils (see Basics)
1-1/2 teaspoons salt
1/2 teaspoon freshly ground
    black pepper
reserved red beans and any
    liquid
1 cup long-grain rice
Bring to gentle boil, cover and
simmer 1 hour. Last 15 minutes
of cooking add:
3 medium beets, cooked and cut
    into small julienne
2 cups each chopped Swiss
    chard and spinach
more liquid (water or stock)
    if desired
salt, pepper, turmeric and
    cayenne pepper to taste
Just before serving add and cook
3 to 4 minutes to blend flavors:
1/4 cup lemon juice
Serve in large bowls and pass:
plain yoghurt for topping
Serves 6 to 8 as main meal

PERSIAN CAT
(OUTRAGEOUS)

*It is generally hypothesized
that the Angora long-haired cat
was so designated because of
some distant acquaintance with
Ankara, Turkey, which does not
sufficiently explain why it is here
in the Persian chapter bearing
the title of Persian cat.*

LENTIL AND SPINACH PILAF

Sauté until spinach is wilted in:
3 tablespoons butter
1 bunch spinach, washed, dried
  and chopped
1 garlic clove, minced
Add:
1-1/2 cups cooked lentils
  (see Basics)
1 tablespoon chopped parsley
1/2 teaspoon salt
1/4 teaspoon each pepper and
  cumin
Sauté just until ingredients are
blended and heated through,
about 4 or 5 minutes. Do not
overcook. Adjust seasonings to
taste. Place on heated platter and
pour over pilaf:
3 tablespoons melted butter
Serves 4

OUTRAGEOUS PERSIAN CAT

PERSIA

STUFFED ZUCCHINI WITH APRICOTS

Halve crosswise and then lengthwise:

2 large zucchini (approximately 12 ounces each)

Scoop out pulp, leaving a shell approximately 3/4 inch thick. Chop pulp and reserve. Parboil shells 2 to 3 minutes in:

boiling salted water

Drain, dry, sprinkle with salt and pepper and set aside. Sauté until onion is transparent in:

3 tablespoons butter
1 onion, minced
half the chopped reserved zucchini pulp

Add:

1 cup long-grain rice
1 cup water
1 large ripe tomato, peeled and chopped
1/2 teaspoon salt
1/4 teaspoon each sugar, cinnamon and black pepper

Cook and stir 15 minutes to blend flavors and partially cook rice. Adjust to taste. Stuff zucchini and set aside. Boil until soft:

1-1/2 cups diced dried apricots
2 cups water
1 to 2 tablespoons honey
1/4 teaspoon cinnamon

Layer half the apricots and juices in baking pan. Place zucchini on top and spoon rest of mixture over. Sprinkle with:

1 tablespoon lemon juice

Bake in 350° oven, basting several times, 30 minutes. Serve hot or at room temperature.

Serves 4 to 6

STUFFED APPLES

Cut 1 inch off tops of:

4 tart cooking apples

Scoop out pulp, leaving 1/4-inch shell. Reserve shells. Chop pulp and cook, covered, until barely tender in:

1/4 cup water

Remove cover and let moisture cook away. To half the pulp add:

1/2 cup cooked lentils (see Basics)
1/2 cup steamed rice (see Basics), using water
1/3 cup raisins
1 cup minced onions, browned in
3 tablespoons butter
1/2 teaspoon salt
1/4 teaspoon each turmeric and black pepper
1/8 teaspoon cumin

Mix well and adjust seasonings to taste. Stuff apples and set aside.

Combine reserved pulp with:

1/2 cup raisins
2 teaspoons sugar

Place mixture in bottom of a small, shallow buttered casserole. Arrange apples, touching, on top. Dot each with:

butter

Bake in 300° oven 45 minutes or until apples are tender and rice stuffing is heated through. Just before serving sprinkle with:

paprika

Serves 4 as luncheon or side dish; 2 as main course

CHELO
(Also Chello, Chilau)

Although this dish is traditionally made with Persian basmati rice, this rice is imported here only in small quantities, and is therefore difficult to find. Our long-grain rice may be substituted to make this unusual dish.

Cover with water and soak 6 to 8 hours:
1-1/2 cups basmati or long-grain rice, well washed
1 tablespoon salt
Rinse rice well and gradually add it to:
2 quarts boiling water
1 tablespoon salt
Boil rapidly 8 minutes or until almost tender.
In heavy saucepan melt:
4 tablespoons butter
2 tablespoons hot water
Mound rice in saucepan, forming into a cone shape. Make a hole in the center of the cone down to bottom of pan and pour into the hole:
4 tablespoons melted butter

Wrap lid of saucepan in tea towel to prevent condensation, cover saucepan and cook over low to medium-low heat 35 minutes or until rice is fluffy and crust has formed on bottom. Place saucepan in cold water for 2 minutes. Serve the rice with:
extra pats of butter
1 egg yolk per serving
sprinkling of powdered sumac*
The crusty portion of the rice may be served separately. To use for garnish, mound all but 2/3 cup of the rice on heated serving platter. To reserved rice add:
pinch saffron, or
1/4 cup finely diced ripe peeled tomato
Surround mound of rice with mixture for color and garnish. Chelo is traditionally served with slices of lamb that have been marinated in lemon juice and grated onion for up to 3 days, and then charcoal broiled. Provide side dishes of yoghurt and a salad of chopped green onion tops dressed with an anise-flavored dressing.
Serves 4 to 6
*Sumac is an herb of the mint family. Available in Middle Eastern stores.

COUCOU

This is also called kuku. It is like an Italian frittata.

Sauté until tender in:
3 tablespoons butter
2/3 cup chopped white of leeks
1 large onion, finely sliced
Lower fire and with spatula pat mixture firmly onto bottom of skillet. Top with:
1 large baking potato, peeled and thinly sliced
2 ripe tomatoes, peeled and thinly sliced
Sprinkle with:
2 tablespoons minced fresh basil
1/4 cup each minced parsley and green pepper
1/2 teaspoon salt
1/4 teaspoon pepper
Dot with:
2 tablespoons butter, cut into bits
Pour over vegetables:
8 eggs, beaten
Cover and simmer over low fire until eggs are set and top is golden. Omelet will puff up and then fall. Remove from fire and invert carefully onto heated platter. Garnish with:
tomato wedges
parsley sprigs
Serves 4

PERSIA

AASHAK
(Leek Ravioli with Yoghurt and Meat Sauce)

This recipe was given to me by Mr. and Mrs. Anwar Hfzali of the Shah restaurant in Manhattan Beach, California.

To make dough, sift into bowl:
3 cups sifted white flour
1-1/4 teaspoons salt
Add to form very stiff dough:
1 cup minus 2 tablespoons
    cold water
Knead until very smooth and divide into 3 balls. Cover with tea towel and let rest at least 30 minutes.
To make filling, combine:
5 to 6 cups chopped white of
    leeks
2-1/2 tablespoons vegetable oil
2-1/2 teaspoons salt
1 teaspoon paprika
1/2 teaspoon cayenne pepper
Working with half a ball of dough at a time and keeping rest of dough covered, roll 1/16 inch thick, adding flour as needed. If using a noodle machine, knead on #8, cut in half, put through #4 twice and then #3 twice. Cut into 2-inch rounds and place on rounds about 1 teaspoon of leek filling. Fold over and moisten edges to seal tightly. As you work, place ravioli on cookie sheet and keep covered with tea towel. Each ball of dough should make about 50 rounds. Repeat with rest of dough and scraps and filling and refrigerate (or freeze no more than 2 days).

Meat Sauce
In heavy skillet heat:
1/2 cup vegetable oil
Add and brown:
2-1/2 cups minced onion
Gradually add, stirring with fork to brown meat:
1-1/2 pounds ground lean beef,
    crumbled
1 teaspoon salt
1/2 teaspoon black pepper
Blend in:
3/4 cup tomato juice
3 cups water
Bring to boil and cook over medium heat, stirring often, until liquid evaporates and sauce is oily (about 40 minutes). Toward end of cooking time, stir constantly. Push a bit of meat aside and sprinkle with a little water. If oil sizzles most of the water has been cooked away. Adjust seasonings.
Cool, cover and refrigerate if making ahead.

Yoghurt Sauce (Chaka)
Combine:
3 cups yoghurt (if using home-
    made yoghurt, strain enough
    to make 2 cups)
4 garlic cloves, mashed or
    finely minced
1-1/2 teaspoons salt
Adjust to taste and refrigerate until ready to assemble the aashak. Bring to boil:
2 to 3 quarts water
1 teaspoon each salt and vege-
    table oil
Drop 2 dozen or so ravioli into boiling water, lower heat slightly and cook 5 to 8 minutes. Remove to colander to drain and repeat with rest of ravioli. (Cooked ravioli may be kept hot after draining in heavy saucepan, covered and set over very low heat.) Do not overcook. To assemble the aashak:
Reheat meat sauce. Place half the chaka on large platter and cover with ravioli. Pour rest of chaka over and sprinkle with:
1 tablespoon naunau (ground
    dry mint), or
1/4 cup finely minced fresh mint
Top with meat sauce and serve immediately.
Serves 8

PERSIAN "IMMORTAL"

When Alexander came to Persepolis, the Persian army consisted of all the able-bodied men, numbering one-quarter of the entire population. Ten thousand of these troops were known as "immortals," highly skilled in the martial sciences. This one is indeed immortalized in stone on a wall in Persepolis, standing at ready to defend his King, the great Darius.

LAMB AND APRICOT CHELO

In heavy skillet sauté until tender in:
4 tablespoons butter
3 onions, finely minced
Push aside and brown well on all sides:
3 pounds boneless lamb stew meat, cubed
Add and sauté 5 minutes to blend flavors:
2 cups dried apricots
1 cup seedless raisins
additional butter if needed
Cover with:
lamb or chicken broth
Stir well, cover, lower heat and simmer, stirring occasionally and adding broth as needed, 2 hours. In this time sauce should be quite thick and flavors blended. Last half hour of cooking add:
juice of 1/2 lemon
1/2 cup prune juice
3 tablespoons apricot preserves
Remove 12 apricots from pan juices, transfer lamb and juices and fruits to heated platter and garnish with:
reserved apricots
Serve with chelo (page 43).
Serves 6

PERSIA

KABULI PALAU
(Lamb Shank Pilaf)

This recipe was given to me by Mr. and Mrs. Anwar Hfzali from the Shah restaurant in Manhattan Beach, California. Among their palaus, this I find reigns as the favorite with my guests.
I have taken the liberty of a few changes, substituting lamb shanks for the lamb cubes.

Brown on all sides in a Dutch oven:
3 tablespoons butter or salad oil
4 small lamb shanks, cracked
Remove and set aside. In same pan, sauté until tender, adding more butter if needed:
2 onions, minced
2 garlic cloves, minced
Add and stir well:
1 teaspoon each allspice and cumin
1/2 teaspoon each cardamom and salt
1/4 teaspoon each pepper and powdered saffron
Return lamb shanks to pan and add water to cover. Cover pan and simmer over low heat until shanks are tender. Remove shanks and keep warm. In separate skillet cook covered until carrots are tender:
46

4 small young carrots, cut into long slivers
1 cup almonds
1 cup seedless raisins
1 tablespoon sugar
water as needed
Set aside and prepare rice.
Gradually stir into:
3 cups boiling water combined with 1 cup juices from lamb
2 cups long-grain rice
Bring back to gentle boil, stir, cover and over very low heat cook 20 minutes.
Combine carrot mixture with:
remaining juices from lamb
Reheat, remove shanks to serving platter and pour half the sauce over. Mound rice in heated serving platter and pour rest of sauce over. Top lamb and rice with:
1/2 cup blanched almonds, fried in butter
Serves 4 to 6
The Syrian stuffed apples complement this dish, either hot with the rice or cold as a dessert.

FESENJAN
(Duck in Walnut and Pomegranate Sauce)

Wash, pat dry and quarter:
1 4- to 5-pound duck
Rub well with:
salt and pepper
Gently brown duck on all sides, pricking the skin while cooking, in:
4 tablespoons butter
Duck is fatty and will release fat when cooking. Remove duck to Dutch oven and set aside. In separate skillet sauté until golden and tender in:
4 tablespoons butter
2 onions, grated
Lower fire, stir mixture and add:
2 cups finely pulverized walnuts
1/2 cup pomegranate syrup or juice
3 tablespoons sugar
1 teaspoon cardamom
1/2 teaspoon salt
1/4 teaspoon pepper
2-1/2 cups water
1 tablespoon lemon juice
Cook over low heat until well blended. Pour over duck; turn duck so that it is completely covered with sauce.
Cover and cook over low fire 45 minutes or until tender,

basting several times during cooking and skimming off any fat that appears on the surface of sauce. Remove duck to heated platter and pour pan sauce over. Sprinkle with:
3/4 cup chopped walnuts
Garnish with:
tangerine sections
Serve with:
chelo (page 43)
Serves 4

Note: When fresh pomegranates are in season they add an exotic touch. Add to sauce while duck is cooking and combine the seeds with the walnuts to sprinkle over.

Variations
Substitute chicken for the duck, reducing cooking time and adding to sauce:
1/2 teaspoon grated orange rind
Or leave duck whole, stuff with pilaff and brown in 400° oven. Reduce heat to 300°, pour sauce over and roast, basting often and skimming off fat that forms on top of sauce, approximately 2 hours. Remove duck to serving platter, scoop out stuffing and serve separately. Serve duck with sauce poured over and garnish with fresh fruit slices. Serve extra sauce in a bowl.

TILE FROM THE BLUE MOSQUE OF SHAH JEHAN IN TABRIZ, PERSIA

47

PERSIA

BROILED STURGEON

Cut into 1-1/2-inch chunks:
2 pounds sturgeon
Marinate 20 minutes in mixture of:
3 tablespoons olive oil
**2 tablespoons each lemon juice
  and minced fresh dill weed**
Drain and reserve marinade.
Skewer and sprinkle liberally with:
paprika
Broil, basting often with reserved marinade, 10 minutes, turning once, or until tender. Do not overcook. Serve with lentil and spinach pilaf.
Serves 4

AJIL VENDOR ON PAVEMENT IN SMALL CASPIAN TOWN

AJIL VENDOR ON
PAVEMENT IN
SMALL CASPIAN TOWN

*Ajil is a collective word for
a variety of foods such as one
might incorporate into a granola
recipe. Grains, nuts, dates, raisins,
and the like are weighed out on
the fellow's scales, as well as
fish and certain sweetmeats.*

APRICOT DELIGHT

In saucepan combine:
1 cup dried apricots
1-1/2 cups water
2 tablespoons apricot preserves
1/3 cup sugar
3 slivers lemon peel
1/2 teaspoon grated orange peel
Bring to gentle boil and simmer
25 minutes until mixture is soft
and syrupy. Cool and purée in
blender. Whip until stiff:
1 cup heavy cream
Gently fold into apricot mixture
and spoon into sherbet glasses.
Chill and serve with:
topping of slightly sweetened
**   whipped cream**
sprinkling of chopped pistachios
Serves 4 to 6

FRUIT MOLD

For a truly exotic dessert, prepare
this cake embedded with fruit
and surrounded with a ring of
whipped cream garnished with
whole strawberries.

Sift together and set aside:
1 cup sifted cake flour
1 teaspoon baking powder
1/4 teaspoon salt
Beat until stiff:
4 egg whites
Add and beat until well mixed:
4 egg yolks, beaten
2 tablespoons almond paste
1 cup sugar
1 tablespoon lukewarm water
1 teaspoon freshly grated
**   orange rind**
Slowly add the sifted ingredients
to the egg mixture and set aside.
Whip until it stands in stiff peaks:
1 pint whipping cream
Add to whipped cream, blending
in thoroughly:
2 tablespoons imported quince
**   preserves**
Refrigerate until ready to use.
Have ready:
3 slices fresh pineapple
4 large whole strawberries
8 apricots, pitted and halved
16 pitted cherries
1 cup seedless grapes

Generously butter a large ring
fruit mold. Firmly press the
pineapple slices into mold indentations. Arrange between the
slices 8 apricot halves and 8
cherries around the halves. Pour
half of the cake batter evenly
over fruit. Spoon on half of the
whipped cream and smooth it
evenly over the batter. Stud the
whipped cream with 4 strawberries, tip down, firmly
secured. Cover with remaining
cake batter. Arrange the remaining fruit on top of the batter and
place mold on a cookie sheet.
Bake in a 350° oven for approximately 35 minutes, or until
a toothpick inserted in cake
comes out clean. Cool slightly
and invert cake on a serving plate.
Using a pastry tube, surround
the cake with the reserved
whipped cream. Place on the
whipped cream:
4 whole unhulled strawberries
Serves 8 to 10

WOMAN OF CENTRAL TURKEY

TURKEY

THE MOUNTAINOUS peninsula jutting westward between Europe and Africa—between the Black Sea and the Mediterranean—has been ignominiously named "Asia Minor" by geographers, but its place in history and in man's imagination is anything but minor. Here mighty empires and great cities have been born, destroyed and reborn; cataclysmic battles have been fought for political and religious control of its diverse peoples; the arts and sciences have alternately flourished and languished, while the art of living together seems to be in the same experimental stage it was in when the Hittites arrived from the northeast nearly 4000 years ago. Today the Turks, descended from Central Asian nomads, dominate the fiercely independent Kurds who failed in their attempt to set up a separate country where modern Turkey joins Syria and Iraq. The Laz, Turkoman, Georgian and Circassian peoples constitute other minorities in what might be called a still boiling cauldron of history.

In a fertile plain along the northwest coast archeologists have discovered remains of nine cities, each built on top of the ruins of another. Troy I, the oldest and deepest with crude brick walls, dates back to the Early Bronze Age (about 3000 B.C.). Material from Troy VI, destroyed by earthquake about 1300 B.C., was used to build Troy VII, which was burned and plundered before 1200 B.C.—according to legend by the soldiers of the Trojan horse. Troy VIII was a small village, while Troy IX became the Greco-Roman city of Ilium lasting until the 300's A.D.

By far the most famous city, the one that still straddles the Bosporus straits into the Black Sea, was founded by Greek adventurers in the early 500's B.C. who named it Byzantium. Darius made it part of his Persian empire in 513 B.C. Then in the 300's B.C. came Alexander the Great, to be followed not long after by the Romans. With the split in the Roman Empire and the fall of Rome, Byzantium assumed the role of the center of culture in the Mediterranean world. By the 300's A.D. Emperor Constantine had already enlarged this Eastern capital, calling it "New Rome," though it later became known as Constantinople in his honor. Byzantine art and architecture date back to churches built here in 450 A.D.

TURKEY

Although briefly conquered by the Crusaders in 1203 and 1204, this sparkling jewel of a city withstood repeated attacks of invaders until 1453, when it fell to the Turks, a branch of the Aschin Huns, who controlled Central Asia from 552 to 650. Constantinople became Istanbul. Meanwhile, most of the Byzantine Empire had felt the hand and the new religion of the Arabs in the 600's A.D., the might of the Turks as early as 1071, and the cruel destruction of the Mongols in 1300.

Byzantine food, always different from that of Rome, has many legacies: its own famous yellow figs of Izmir (Smyrna), Oriental spices, sliced meat from the Caucasus to the north, over 100 fresh seafoods of the Bosporus, cakes from Egypt, black truffles from Arabian deserts and dates from the oases, *couscous* from the Maghreb, Frankish-style roast lamb from the West, rice cooked in milk from India, *maghmuma* (layered dish of mutton, onions, and eggplant—forerunner of *moussaka*) from the East. Turkish warriors roasting chunks of mutton *(kebab)* skewered on a sword *(sis)* over campfires contributed shish kebab, and their leaders added to Byzantine culture a predilection for the voluptuous life.

Circassian beauties were purchased for sultans' harems. Feasts became lavish rituals. Frothing narrow pots of strong, black coffee were made from freshly roasted green beans, pulverized and quickly steeped in boiling water. After sweetening, the inky brew—froth, grounds and all—was poured into tiny cups and sipped while piping hot. Though the Turks embraced Islam, they have long countenanced occasional sipping of *raki,* a strong, anise-flavored liquor. Another delightful thirst-quencher is *ayran,* a diluted, salted yoghurt.

The Turkish Moslems who could afford it sought their paradise in the present, not the hereafter. Their *houris* were luscious, live beauties, not angels in heaven, dancing erotically or serving *baklava* dripping with honey at sumptuous feasts where food was served in a communal bowl on a low table surrounded by cushions. The poet Revānī in *Isret Nāme* wrote of banquets of "rice like pearls, saffron dishes like yellow-haired beauties, and *gada'if* [*konafa*—a sweet pastry] like silver-bodied lovelings." Even today some pastries bear such names as "sweethearts' lips" and "lady's navel."

The Turkey of subservient women, whirling dervishes, dancing harem girls, fezzes, ancient dining customs and elaborate *houkahs* has changed. Kemel Attaturk, the determined ruler who took over in 1923, westernized and modernized Turkey by separating church and state, moving the capital to Ankara, abolishing harems and introducing brimmed hats for men. Today Turkey is considered the most modern country in the Middle East. Voluptuous living for the few has given way to better education and a better life for the many. Traditions and customs long considered sacred have fallen by the wayside, but, luckily, many of the foods, artifacts and architectural masterpieces of Turkey's rich past survive for modern man to enjoy and savor. Foods such as tomatoes and green peppers from the New World, like adopted Western ideas, add a new sheen to the patina of the past.

ISTANBUL AT EVENTIDE FROM THE GALATA BRIDGE

GALATA BRIDGE

This is the famous tourist bridge at sunset, when the light is reflected from the already set sun off the sky, and then off the water. At times like this, the city of Istanbul is in silhouette and the sky is brilliant orange.

CHICKEN BÖREK

Böreks, paper-thin pastry filled with meat or vegetables, are very popular snacks in Turkey. This Turkish börek is the most delectable of all. It may be served as an appetizer or an exciting brunch dish.

Combine:
1 whole chicken breast, boiled, skinned, boned and minced
1-1/2 cups Béchamel sauce (see Basics)
1/2 teaspoon each salt and paprika
2 egg yolks
1 cup shredded unsweetened coconut
1/2 cup seedless raisins
1/4 teaspoon cinnamon
Have ready:
6 phyllo sheets (see Basics)
Butter each sheet as directed, stack and place chicken mixture on short end 2 inches from sides.

Roll once, fold in sides and roll like jelly roll. Place seam side down on buttered cookie sheet, brush with melted butter and bake in 300° oven 40 minutes or until golden. Cool slightly and cut into 1-inch slices.
Makes approximately 16 appetizer servings
For brunch, serve hot and cover with:
Béchamel sauce (see Basics)
cooked peas
Serve with tossed green salad with yoghurt dressing.
Serves 6 for brunch

53

TURKEY

STUFFED MUSSELS APPETIZER

Soak 2 hours in:
salted water to cover
2 dozen large mussels
Scrub thoroughly and place in steamer with:
1/2 cup each water and white wine
2 garlic cloves, mashed
4 sprigs parsley
1/2 lemon, sliced
Bring to boil and steam 5 minutes or until mussels open. Discard any mussels that do not open. Remove from heat, cool and remove 6 mussels from shells. Reserve shells and mince the 6 mussels. Set aside with remaining mussels. Strain liquid and add to make 2 cups in all:
clam juice
In heavy saucepan sauté until tender in:
3 tablespoons olive oil
1 cup minced green onions
Add, stir well and bring to boil:
reserved mussel liquid and clam juice
1 cup rice
Cover and simmer 20 minutes.

Remove from heat and with fork toss in:
1/2 cup each pine nuts and currants
3 tablespoons finely chopped parsley
1 garlic clove, minced
1 teaspoon allspice
additional olive oil as needed for moisture
minced reserved mussels
Set aside. Over each remaining mussel in shell sprinkle:
lemon juice
Mound rice mixture onto mussels in shells and fill empty shells with remaining rice mixture. Place side by side in shallow baking dish and drizzle over all:
olive oil
Bake in 300° oven 10 minutes or until heated through and bubbly. Serve on platter garnished with:
lemon wedges
parsley sprigs
Serve each guest a mussel with stuffing and a shell with stuffing.
Makes 18 individual servings

TRIPE AND RICE SOUP

In lightly salted water parboil 15 minutes:
1-1/2 pounds tripe
Drain, discarding water, and rinse in cold water. Cut into 1/2-inch dice and in large pot combine with:
3 quarts water
1 cup raw rice
1 teaspoon oregano
1/2 teaspoon cumin
1 or more chili peppers, chopped
1 bay leaf
Bring to boil, lower heat and cook 1-1/2 hours or until tripe is tender and rice is soft and smooth. Broth should be thick and creamy. Sauté until transparent and lightly golden in:
2 tablespoons olive oil
1 onion, chopped
3 to 4 tablespoons finely minced garlic
Do not brown. Add to soup pot and continue cooking 20 minutes. Just before serving slowly drizzle in, stirring constantly:
2 eggs beaten with
1/4 cup lemon juice
Season to taste with:
salt and freshly ground black pepper
Serves 6 to 8 as main dish soup

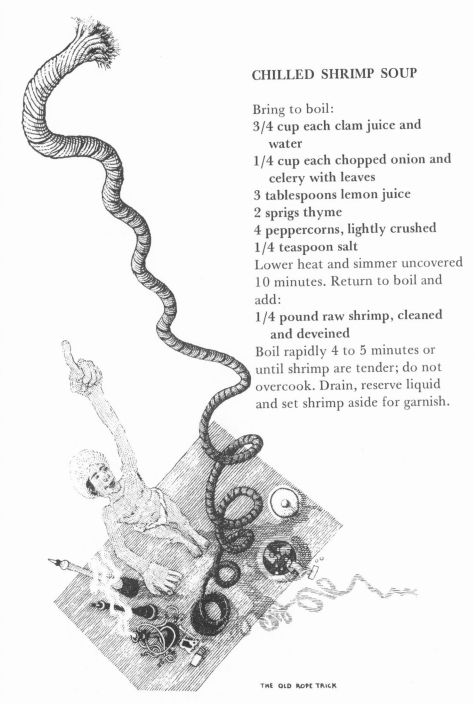

THE OLD ROPE TRICK

CHILLED SHRIMP SOUP

Bring to boil:

3/4 cup each clam juice and water

1/4 cup each chopped onion and celery with leaves

3 tablespoons lemon juice

2 sprigs thyme

4 peppercorns, lightly crushed

1/4 teaspoon salt

Lower heat and simmer uncovered 10 minutes. Return to boil and add:

1/4 pound raw shrimp, cleaned and deveined

Boil rapidly 4 to 5 minutes or until shrimp are tender; do not overcook. Drain, reserve liquid and set shrimp aside for garnish.

To reserved liquid add:

2 cups milk

1 pound raw shrimp, cleaned, deveined and minced

6 parsley sprigs

1/4 teaspoon nutmeg

1/4 teaspoon freshly ground white pepper

Bring to gentle boil, cover and simmer over low heat, stirring occasionally, 30 minutes. Cool slightly and purée in blender. Force through sieve if completely smooth soup is desired.

Return to saucepan and add:

2 egg yolks, beaten with

1 cup heavy cream

Cook and stir until slightly thickened. Cool and add:

1-1/2 cups finely minced cucumber (salted, drained and patted dry)

Chill thoroughly and adjust seasonings to taste with:

lemon juice

salt

freshly ground white pepper

Serve in chilled bowls and garnish each bowl with:

reserved shrimp

thinly sliced lemon

minced parsley or dill

Serves 4 to 6

TURKEY

MUEZZIN PROCLAIMING
AZAN, CALL TO ONE OF FIVE
WORSHIP PERIODS DAILY
IN ISTANBUL

ORANGE AND ONION SALAD

Peel and slice:
2 sweet oranges
Arrange on lettuce leaves
alternately with:
**2 medium sweet onions, thinly
  sliced**
Top with:
black olive halves
Combine and pour over salad:
3 tablespoons olive oil mixed with
1 tablespoon lemon juice
Serves 4

MUEZZIN CALLING AZAN

*Five times each day, Azan is
called and the faithful turn
toward Mecca and pray. This
practice is initiated by the
muezzin high in a minaret,
beginning the worship. Frequently, this ancient practice
is given a 20th century electronic
boost by the use of bull horns
or amplified public-address
systems.*

BULGHUR PILAFF

Though rice is popular in Turkey, the mainstay of a Turk's diet is bulghur.

In heavy skillet lightly brown over high heat in:
4 tablespoons butter
3/4 cup minced onion
Add, stir well and brown slightly:
2 cups bulghur
Add and bring to boil:
4 cups hot chicken broth
Stir, mixing well, cover and steam over low heat 20 minutes. Remove from heat, let stand 5 minutes and fluff with fork. Mound on heated platter and serve immediately.
Serves 4

BAYRAM IC PILAV
(Turkish Holiday Pilav in Phyllo)

Brown gently in:
1/4 pound butter
1 cup long-grain rice
1 medium-size onion, grated
1/4 cup pine nuts
Add, combine well and bring to gentle boil:

2 cups chicken broth
2 medium-size tomatoes, peeled and chopped
2 tablespoons currants
1/2 teaspoon allspice or cinnamon
1/2 teaspoon sugar
1/4 teaspoon each salt and pepper
Cover and simmer 20 minutes until rice is tender and moisture is absorbed.
Sauté until cooked through in:
2 tablespoons butter
4 chicken livers, halved
Cool and chop livers. Toss into rice mixture with:
1/2 cup Béchamel sauce (see Basics)
Cool and set aside. Butter as directed (see Basics):
8 sheets phyllo
Place in buttered 9-inch round baking pan, to form a shell, buttering between each layer. Bake in 350° oven 10 minutes until golden. Cool slightly and fill with rice mixture, pressing in gently. Bake in 300° oven 10 minutes. Invert shell onto baking sheet. Raise heat to 350° and continue baking until phyllo is golden. Let cool 10 minutes before cutting into wedges with very sharp knife.
Serves 6 to 8

SULTAN'S PILAFF

In a heavy skillet, sauté until grains are thoroughly coated in:
1/2 pound butter
3 cups rice
Combine and heat:
6 cups beef broth
3/4 teaspoon allspice
pinch of saffron
salt and freshly ground pepper to taste
Add heated broth to rice, stir well, cover, lower heat and cook until moisture is absorbed and rice is fluffy. Toss into rice:
1/3 cup sultanas
1/4 cup coarsely chopped pistachios
Cover and set aside 5 minutes. Toss with forks and form the pilaff into a mound on a heated serving platter. Sprinkle on top:
2 tablespoons coarsely chopped, toasted pistachios
Serves 12

TURKEY

STUFFED POTATOES

Scrub well and dry:

6 large baking potatoes

Cut a slice off one end of each potato and stand upright in well-buttered shallow baking dish. Bake in 350° oven 40 minutes or until soft. Cut off 1-1/2-inch tops and set aside for another use. Carefully scoop out inside of potato, leaving a shell approximately 1/2 inch thick. Reserve shells and mash or rice the potato. Beat into potato:

4 tablespoons butter, softened

2 chicken breasts, boiled, skinned, boned and minced

1 cup minced mushrooms, sautéed in

1 tablespoon butter

2 tablespoons minced parsley

2/3 cup half-and-half or enough to make smooth consistency

1/4 teaspoon nutmeg

salt and pepper to taste

Fill potato shells with mixture and place on top of each potato:

pat of butter

button mushroom

Stand closely in buttered baking dish and bake in 450° oven 15 to 20 minutes. Last 10 minutes heat any extra stuffing in oven. When potatoes have finished baking, brush with melted butter and roll

58

in chopped parsley. Mound extra stuffing in center of heated serving platter and surround with potatoes. Sprinkle mound with:

cooked peas

Serve with:

yoghurt

Serves 6

STUFFED GREEN PEPPERS

Boil 5 minutes and cool:

8 green peppers

Cut off tops and reserve tops. Remove seeds from peppers and set aside.

Sauté until browned in:

3 tablespoons butter

1 large onion, chopped

Add and bring to gentle boil:

1-1/2 cups bulghur or rice

1/2 cup each pine nuts and currants

3 tablespoons minced parsley

1/4 teaspoon dried basil

1 teaspoon minced fresh mint

1 teaspoon salt

1/2 teaspoon freshly ground black pepper

1 16-ounce can tomatoes

1 cup water

Cover, lower heat and cook gently 20 minutes, adding just before rice is tender:

1 teaspoon brown sugar

Fill reserved peppers with mixture, replace tops and stand peppers in heavy skillet, brushing each lavishly with:

olive oil

Add to skillet:

1 cup water

Cover and steam 20 minutes or until tender. Remove to serving platter and chill.

Serves 4 as main dish, 8 as vegetable accompaniment

TOPKAPI TREASURE SULTAN

This gift of the Maharaja of India to the Sultan of Turkey is indeed unique. The pillars and canopy are carved glass as is the base, which also has other valuable substances in it. The fringe and mast tops are gold laden with rubies, sapphires and emeralds. The grapes in the Sultan's dish are diamonds, and precious gems decorate the entire creation. The Sultan himself, seated on his pillow with his Sunday turban on his head, is carved from a single pearl.

TOPKAPI PEARL SULTAN ❋ 19TH CENTURY

TURKEY

FAMILIAR 16ᵗʰ CENTURY TURK DESIGN

IMAM BAYELDI

Cut in half lengthwise:
8 Japanese eggplants
Make 2 deep slashes in pulp of
each half. Sprinkle with salt and
let stand in colander to drain.
Sauté until onion is softened in:
1/2 cup olive oil
4 large onions, thinly sliced
   in rings
Add:
4 garlic cloves, cut in slivers
6 medium-size ripe tomatoes,
   peeled, seeded and coarsely
   chopped
1 teaspoon salt
1/2 teaspoon pepper
1/2 cup minced parsley
Adjust seasonings. Brush baking
pan with oil and place eggplant
halves side by side in pan. Stuff
each slash with as much onion
mixture as possible and fill halves
with remaining mixture.
Place on top of each half:
2 slivers garlic
Pour into pan:
1 cup water
Drizzle over eggplant halves:
2 tablespoons olive oil
Bake in 350° oven 45 minutes or
until eggplant is tender. Remove
to platter, chill and serve cold.
Serves 8

MOUSSAKA À LA TURK

Moussaka is a Greek dish with numerous versions extending throughout the Middle East. The Turkish recipe is baked in a charlotte mold and is a culinary masterpiece requiring great patience, but the results will bring you great accolades. I have used a bundt pan which enhances the beauty of this dish.

In heavy skillet sauté cut side down over medium heat until tender in:
4 tablespoons olive oil, or as needed
4 large eggplants, halved lengthwise
Cool, scoop out pulp, being careful to leave skins intact, chop pulp finely and set pulp and skins aside.
In same skillet, brown:
2 pounds ground lean lamb or beef
1 large onion, minced
2 garlic cloves, minced
2 tablespoons minced parsley
1 teaspoon salt
1/2 teaspoon pepper

Add and combine well:
reserved eggplant pulp
1 16-ounce can tomatoes
1/2 cup chicken or lamb stock
1/4 teaspoon nutmeg
Cook and stir 5 minutes, cool slightly and beat in:
2 eggs, beaten
Adjust seasonings to taste and set aside. Line sides and bottom of a lavishly buttered bundt pan with reserved eggplant skins, purple side out, arranging them to fill the grooves of the pan, slightly overlapping and leaving enough skin to be folded over the top. Pour in half the meat mixture and sprinkle with:
1/4 cup bread crumbs
1/3 cup grated Kefalotyri or Parmesan cheese
Repeat layers, fold skins over to cover entirely and place in larger pan of hot water. Bake in 375° oven 45 minutes or until firm. Let stand 5 minutes, turn out onto heated platter and surround with garnish of:
cherry tomatoes
parsley sprigs
Serve with choice of:
tomato sauce (following)
Béchamel sauce (see Basics)

TOMATO SAUCE

Sauté until soft in:
1/2 cup olive oil
2 onions, minced
2 garlic cloves, minced
1/2 cup finely chopped green pepper
Add:
4 large ripe tomatoes, peeled and chopped, or
1 16-ounce can whole tomatoes
1 6-ounce can tomato paste
Stir and cook slowly 10 minutes. Add and continue cooking and stirring over low heat until thickened:
1 bay leaf, crumbled
1/2 teaspoon each salt and allspice
1/4 teaspoon freshly ground black pepper
2 tablespoons chopped parsley
1/2 teaspoon dried oregano
1 teaspoon sugar (optional)
1 cup chicken broth or water
Adjust seasonings to taste.
Makes approximately 3 cups

TURKEY

KÖFTE
(Meatmold à la Turk)

Here is my version of a Turkish meat loaf.

Follow preceding directions for treating eggplants in Moussaka à la Turk. Reserve eggplant for salad and line a well-buttered bundt pan with eggplant skins, being sure to place skins so they will overlap to cover top of mold. Combine well:

3 pounds lean lamb or sirloin of beef, ground twice
2 onions, grated
2 cups seasoned croutons, soaked in milk or stock and squeezed dry
1/2 cup each minced parsley and minced green pepper
2 garlic cloves, minced
2 eggs, beaten
1/2 cup grated Kefalotyri or Parmesan cheese
3 tablespoons olive oil
1/2 cup tomato sauce
1-1/2 teaspoons salt
1/2 teaspoon freshly ground black pepper

Press meat mixture firmly into the lined mold and fold skins over top. Brush top lavishly with:
melted butter

Place in larger pan of hot water and bake in 350° oven 1 hour. Remove from oven and let stand 5 to 10 minutes. Turn out onto platter and garnish with:
cherry tomatoes
Serve with:
tomato sauce (preceding), or Béchamel sauce (see Basics)
and eggplant salad molded on crisp lettuce and sprinkled with toasted sesame seeds.
Serves 8 to 10

DONER KEBAB

When I met Lambos, a young enterprising chef from Istanbul, we joined forces and opened a bistro called Istanbul on Nob Hill in San Francisco. Later, in 1962, I opened my own restaurant called La Grecque and once more Lambos joined me to introduce for the first time in San Francisco the Turkish doner kebab.

Doner kebab, a combination of marinated slices of lamb, beef and veal, is cooked on a most extraordinary mechanism. The meat slices are attached to an upright spit which slowly turns as the meat cooks from the heat of glowing charcoal, or more recently, an electrical unit. As the spit rotates, a plate with a bed of pilaff is held to receive outside slivers of meat, cut by a deft hand.

Because most people will not have access to this very unusual cooking unit, I offer you my version. Many stoves today have a rotisserie unit which may be used, or one may cook this dish on the rotating spit of a barbecue.

Have ready:
2 sirloin steaks approximately 1 inch thick, cut in half
2 lamb steaks from boneless leg of lamb approximately 3/4 inch thick, cut in half
2 veal steaks from boneless leg of veal approximately 3/4 inch thick, cut in half and flattened slightly
Place meat in shallow pan.
Combine:
2 onions, thinly sliced
2 garlic cloves, minced
2 green peppers, cut in thin rings
juice of 2 lemons
3/4 cup olive oil
1/4 cup minced parsley
1-1/2 teaspoons oregano
3 bay leaves
1/4 teaspoon thyme
2 teaspoons salt
1 teaspoon freshly ground pepper

Pour marinade over meats and turn pieces several times until well coated. Pour over all:

1 cup white wine

Refrigerate marinating meat overnight. String on spit securely, alternating the lamb, beef and veal. If cooking in a stove rotisserie, place a pan beneath the spit to catch the drippings. Or broil about 6 inches above hot coals. Cook, basting frequently with the marinade, approximately 35 minutes, or until meat is cooked to taste and lightly browned. Release meat from skewer onto a heated serving platter to form a loaf. Garnish one side of platter with:

green pepper rings

Cut steak as you would chateaubriand and serve with Sultan's pilaff (page 57).

Serves 12

AFYON, TURKEY'S GOVERNMENT OPIUM FARM

When harvest time comes around, these Turk maidens stroll through the fields and make a slender incision around the equator of the poppy pod. The next day they return with small pallets to scrape the resinous produce from the pods. The substance produces opium, and when refined, heroin and morphine.

AFYON, TURKEY'S GOVERNMENT OPIUM FARM

TURKEY

CURRY ISTANBUL

John Sarandon, restaurateur, just returned from Istanbul with a succulent Turkish curry. He soon will publish his recipes but I prevailed upon him to part with this one. Like many modern Turkish recipes, it utilizes ingredients from Western Europe.

Bring to boil:
1 pint half-and-half
2 cups grated unsweetened
    coconut
Strain, squeeze coconut dry, and reserve coconut and the coconut cream.
Cook until tender in:
well-seasoned chicken broth to
    cover
6 large chicken breasts
Cool, remove breasts and reserve broth. Slice chicken meat into julienne pieces and set aside.
Sauté until soft in:
3 tablespoons butter
2 large onions, chopped
2 garlic cloves, minced
Blend in:
2 tablespoons curry powder or
    to taste
3 tablespoons ground walnuts
Cook and stir 3 minutes and gradually add:

1 cup reserved coconut cream
1 cup reserved chicken broth
Cook and stir until thickened and blend in:
1 teaspoon Dijon-style mustard
1 cup of the reserved grated
    coconut
1/2 cup each chopped dates and
    raisins, both soaked in brandy
    to cover
1 large tart apple, grated
1 8-ounce jar orange marmalade
Bring to gentle boil, cover and simmer, adding chicken broth as needed, 25 minutes. Last 10 minutes add reserved chicken pieces to heat through. Turn out onto large heated platter and surround with:
6 fresh pineapple slices, halved
Sprinkle with:
3/4 cup toasted blanched almonds
remaining reserved grated coconut
Serve with:
pilaff (see Basics), topped with:
pine nuts sautéed in butter
mandarin orange sections,
    drained
Assorted condiments such as:
chutney
toasted blanched almonds
grated coconut
Serves 10 to 12
Sauce is also good over broiled chicken parts.

STUFFED MACKEREL

Scale, clean, wash and dry:
1 2-pound boned mackerel
Sprinkle inside and out with:
salt and pepper
Set aside. Sauté until onions are transparent in:
1 tablespoon olive oil
1 large onion, sliced in rings
2 tablespoons sultanas
1/2 teaspoon freshly grated
    orange peel
pinch of powdered saffron
Stuff fish with mixture. Combine in bowl:
2 large onions, sliced in rings
1/2 cup sultanas
1 tablespoon orange flower water
1 teaspoon each freshly grated
    orange peel and sugar
1/2 teaspoon cinnamon
pinch of powdered saffron
2 tablespoons orange juice
1/4 cup olive oil
Make a bed of mixture in bottom of baking pan. Place stuffed fish on bed. Take a few spoonfuls from bed and baste fish. Bake in 325° oven 45 minutes, or until tender, basting several times during cooking. Transfer fish to heated platter, surround with sauce and garnish with:
lemon wedges
Serves 4

TURKISH SORCEROR

Here a Turkish sorceror peers into his crystal ball to divine what the future holds in store for him.

TURKEY

FIGS IN YOGHURT

This is another of John
Sarandon's recipes.

Peel:
**12 fresh figs (canned may be
substituted; do not peel)**
Make an identation in each fig
and stuff with mixture of:
**1/2 cup chopped blanched
almonds, pistachio nuts and
walnuts in any combination**
Top each stuffed fig with:
1 whole blanched almond
Place side by side in shallow dish
and pour around to almost cover:
**almond brandy, or fruit wine or
liqueur**
Marinate several hours, remove
figs from brandy and set aside.
Combine:
brandy from marinating
1 pint yoghurt
1 tablespoon honey
1/4 teaspoon vanilla extract
Pour mixture into 4 chilled
stemmed compote glasses. Place
3 figs in each bed of yoghurt and
sprinkle lightly with:
crushed blanched almonds
Chill.
Serves 4

LOCUM
(Turkish Delight)

Memories of my childhood return
me to Chicago's Halsted Street,
a street on which lived Greeks,
Turks, all the peoples of the Middle East. Here I was to see an
incomparable shadow show, the
Turkish puppeteers. A taut sheet,
highly lit, formed the backdrop.
Pressed against this sheet were
cardboard figures, animated with
sticks rather than strings, a most
intricate maneuver. The protago-
nist, a pathetic, deformed figure
named Karagiozis, was in search
of love and release from poverty,
and his adventures were inter-
mingled with laughter and tears.
During the summer, these puppet
shows were staged in the back-
yards of coffee houses. We children sat on boxes and stools
watching with great anticipation
our hero's escapades.
I became so enchanted with this
show that my father found me
a discarded set of puppets and
my friends and I banded together
in an attic and presented our own
show. I feel sadness that the children of today cannot be exposed
to this shadow show, where their
eyes would fill with wonderment.
Among my fondest memories of
those days were the elderly gen-
tlemen who sat watching the
performance, smoking their
nagilah (waterpipes) and treating
the children to rounds of sweets.
The favorite was locum, succulent gelatin squares filled with
pistachios and dusted with
powdered sugar.

In saucepan combine:
1 cup each orange juice and water
3 tablespoons lemon juice
1 tablespoon orange flower water
Sprinkle over to soften:
6 envelopes gelatin
Heat to dissolve gelatin and cook
and stir over medium low heat
4 minutes. Add and stir to
dissolve:
2 cups sugar
**1 teaspoon each grated lemon and
orange rind**
Bring to gentle boil and simmer,
stirring occasionally, 15 to 20
minutes. Cool, stirring often, and
pour into a square pan rinsed
with cold water to level of 3/4 to
1 inch. Chill briefly and if desired
fold in:
**1/2 cup finely chopped unsalted
pistachio nuts**
Cover and chill until set. Unmold
and cut into squares. Sprinkle
squares on all sides with:
sifted powdered sugar

HACIVAD AND KARAGIOZIS

The Punch and Judy of the 15th century Ottoman Empire, Hacivad and Karagiozis carried on a socio-political confrontation unabated by the passage of time. Made from sticks and very thin, colored sheets of paper, the puppets are held against a screen lighted from behind and manipulated with sticks. Hacivad, a sinister establishment type, is incessantly trying to put something over on Karagiozis, a swarthy man of the people. Karagiozis, eventually arriving at his wits' end, usually resolves the problem by means of the cudjel. This morality play is popular throughout the Middle East, as well as the rest of the inhabitable earth.

BAKLAVA

This is traditionally baked in a round pan.

Combine and set aside:
2 pounds pistachio nuts, finely chopped
2/3 cup sugar
Follow directions for working with phyllo (see Basics), using:
1 pound phyllo
1 pound sweet butter
One at a time, place 12 sheets on bottom of pan, buttering each profusely. Spread a thin layer of nut mixture on top, cover with a sheet of buttered phyllo, brush with butter and repeat process until all nuts are used. Cover with remaining buttered sheets. With very sharp knife or razor blade cut top layer into triangles. Insert in center of each triangle:
1 whole clove
Bake in 350° oven 45 minutes to 1 hour or until golden.
While baklava is baking bring to boil:

2 cups sugar
1 cup water
1 cup chopped dried apricots
1/4 cup apricot preserves
2 tablespoons fresh lemon juice
1 2-inch stick cinnamon
Stir to dissolve sugar, lower fire and simmer, stirring often, 15 minutes. When thick and syrupy remove from heat. When baklava is baked, immediately pour all but 1/3 cup of syrup over evenly. Allow to cool several hours, pour remaining syrup over and cut into triangles.

A LOVELY ALAWIT WOMAN OF GABRIEL SAADÉS' TOBACCO-CURING ESTABLISHMENT IN THE MOUNTAINS - SYRIA

THE FERTILE CRESCENT

TOGETHER with Jordan and Iraq, Syria and Lebanon lie in what historians call the Fertile Crescent. Here the famous Tigris and Euphrates Rivers meander from the mountains to the Persian Gulf, the Barada River feeds the giant oasis around Damascus, and coastal rains fall along the Mediterranean side of high mountains. A number of smaller rivers provide other areas for growing grain, fruits and vegetables, but characteristically most of the land is too dry or rugged for anything but the limited grazing of sheep and goats.

Like their ancestors the Phoenicians, the Lebanese are lively traders, and in Syria the ancient caravan city of Damascus is still a bustling hub of commerce. Mohammed is said to have refused to enter Damascus, a paradise on earth, preferring to wait for Eternal Paradise.

Marduk, in Assyro-Babylonian mythology, personified the fertilizing action of the waters. It was he who created grain and plants and made things grow, aided by goddesses Misaba (grain) and Geshtin (wine) and the god Tammus (tree). Along with numerous other gods there were inferior creatures with magical powers, the good and bad *genii* familiar to everyone in the *Arabian Nights*. The Phoenicians' *baals* (deities) are frequently referred to in the Bible as an anathema to the Hebrews' one true God, though their temples were emulated by the Israelites. Solomon's temple is believed to have been constructed of the famous cedars of Mt. Lebanon. But it was the Christian religion, and to an even greater extent the Muslim, to which the mixture of Sumerians, Semites, Hittites and mysterious "peoples of the sea" were finally drawn well over 1000 years ago.

Now called the "Arabic hub," this choice area has always been a crossroads and a battleground. Its foods and customs reflect its colorful past. With deceivingly simple ingredients, infinitely varied dishes are prepared to dazzle the eye as well as titillate the palate. The fare of wandering Bedouins is typically Arabian, but in the cities and valleys more elaborate foods prevail. Syrian farmers, given enough water, are said to grow the lushest of fruits and raise the plumpest of sheep. Meals are introduced with a kaleidoscope

THE FERTILE CRESCENT

ABEL'S GRAVE

of tiny appetizers, *mazza,* limited only by the creativity and ingenuity of the cook.

The ubiquitous eggplant, not rich in calories or vitamins, but delicious in combination with other foods and various seasonings, is used in hundreds of different recipes, each claimed to be the very best by its originator. Once considered poisonous, the eggplant originated either in India or South America depending on which book one reads. Mideastern eggplants are generally slimmer and smaller than our fat, pear-shaped varieties. They're more like the 2- to 3-inch "eggs" that gave this plant its name. *Musakka'a* is a favorite dish of eggplant slices layered with seasoned ground lamb.

Traditional foods include special recipes for *sfeeha* (peppery little meat pies), *tahina* (crushed sesame seeds), *hummus* (mashed chick peas), *kibbeh* (lamb paste), and *tabbouleh* (conventional fresh salad to which mint and nutty-flavored *burghul* have been added). To produce *burghul,* wheat grains are boiled until they split, then parched in the sun and ground into the desired coarseness.

Kid and camel may alternate with lamb for meat. The camel hump is considered a delicacy by some, as well as *alya,* the rendered huge tail of the fat-tail sheep. Two Syrian specialties are the desert truffle and a spectacular *kibbeh* (lamb and bulghur pounded together) with seven concentric layers.

Archeologists have found that early Phoenician traders collected fancy bowls and utensils to add to the pomp and ceremony of their feasts. Modern Lebanese, too, believe in turning a meal into a ceremonial feast lasting for hours, especially when they entertain guests at their spectacular tables.

LEBANESE
MISHI WARAQ SILA
(Swiss Chard Dolma)

This dolma has a refreshing taste, especially for vegetarian palates.

Wash and remove stems from:
2 large bunches Swiss chard
Blanch leaves 1 second and set aside. Chop stems finely and layer them in bottom of heavy saucepan. Sprinkle with:
1 tablespoon olive oil
Set aside.
Sauté until tender in:
2 tablespoons olive oil
2 white of leeks, finely chopped
1 cup minced parsley
1 cup minced green onions
Remove leek mixture to bowl and toss in:
2 cups steamed rice made with chicken broth (see Basics)
1 cup freshly cooked garbanzo beans (see Basics), or
1 cup canned garbanzo beans, drained
1 tablespoon minced fresh mint

Spread chard leaves out on board and place about 1 tablespoon filling on stem end. Roll like jelly roll, folding in sides as you roll. Arrange rolls in rows on top of chopped chard stems in saucepan and add:
1 cup or more chicken broth
2 tablespoons lemon juice
Place plate on top to weigh down rolls and bring to gentle boil. Cover and simmer over low fire 25 minutes. Serve hot.
Makes approximately 2 dozen dolmas

HUMMUS BI TAHINI
(Garbanzo Bean Purée)

Mash together and set aside:
1 to 2 garlic cloves
1/2 teaspoon salt
1/4 teaspoon each black pepper and paprika
1/8 teaspoon cayenne pepper
Drain:
2 cups cooked garbanzo beans (see Basics)
Reserve liquid and set aside 1/4 cup beans for garnish. Mash thoroughly or purée remaining beans in blender.

Gradually blend garlic mixture into mashed beans with:
1/2 cup tahini*
1/4 cup lemon juice
reserved liquid as needed to make creamy consistency
Adjust seasonings to taste and spread on serving plate or spoon into serving bowl. Drizzle over:
1 tablespoon olive oil, mixed with
1/2 teaspoon paprika
Sprinkle with:
minced parsley
Or pour over:
3 tablespoons pine nuts, browned in
1 tablespoon butter
Sprinkle with:
paprika
Garnish plate or bowl with:
reserved whole garbanzo beans
parsley sprigs
Serve with:
pita bread (page 132) cut into triangles
Makes approximately 2-1/2 cups
*Sesame-seed paste available in Middle Eastern stores.

THE FERTILE CRESCENT

LEBANESE
LSANAT MATABBLI
(Lamb Tongue Appetizer)

Wash and place in saucepan with:
water to cover
6 to 8 small lamb tongues (about
    1-1/2 pounds)
Add:
1 large onion, quartered
1 garlic clove
2 stalks celery, cut up
1 whole clove
1 bay leaf
2 teaspoons salt
6 peppercorns, lightly crushed
Bring to gentle boil, cover and
simmer until tender. Cool, peel
and slice thinly. Arrange on
serving platter in overlapping
slices. Combine and pour over
tongue:
1/2 cup olive oil
3 tablespoons lemon juice
Chill. Just before serving, pour
over tongue:
tahini dressing (see Basics)
Sprinkle liberally with:
minced parsley
Garnish with:
lemon wedges
Serves 12

LAMP DJINN

72

PICKLED GRAPES

Wash, stem and dry:
approximately 1 pound seedless grapes
Place in hot sterilized wide-mouth 1-pint jar. Bring to boil and remove from heat:
1/2 cup each white vinegar and water
2 teaspoons sugar
1 cinnamon stick
1/2 teaspoon allspice
2 whole cloves
1/2 teaspoon rose water
1/4 cup freshly squeezed orange juice

Pour over grapes to fill jar within 1 inch of top. Seal and let stand 2 days before serving.
Makes 1 pint

LAMP DJINN

This is a bit of artistic license. True enough, there are those Syrians who believe in the Djinni, although there is actually no connection with oil lamps à la Aladdin.
In a 12th century Syrian manuscript, there is a reference to Djinn living on cats, which are subsequently held in high esteem in that land. The description of a single Djinni, which follows this cryptic mention, bears a remarkable reference to the physical appearance of the common flea. It was against holy law to kill a Djinni or its feline host.

LEBANESE PICKLED EGGPLANT WITH WALNUTS

Cook in boiling water until just tender:
4 slender Japanese eggplants approximately 4 inches long, stems removed
Drain well and cut a lengthwise incision to form a pocket. Place on paper and let drain overnight. Combine:
1/2 cup minced walnuts
2 garlic cloves, minced
1 onion, finely minced
Salt the pocket of eggplant and fill with walnut mixture. Place in hot sterilized 1-pint wide-mouth jar. Fill jar to top with:
approximately 1 cup olive oil
Seal tightly and keep in cool place approximately 2 weeks. Serve as appetizer, whole or sliced into 1-inch rings.
Makes 1 pint

VEGETABLE BÖREK

Sauté until soft in:
3 tablespoons butter
1/2 cup minced green onions
Add and brown gently:
chopped boiled giblets from 1 chicken
Add and cook 5 to 10 minutes:
1 cup chopped whites of leeks
1 pound fresh spinach, leaves only, chopped
2 small zucchini, grated
1/4 teaspoon each allspice and pepper
1/2 teaspoon salt
butter as needed
Cool and blend in:
1 egg yolk, lightly beaten
Adjust seasonings and set aside. Following directions for working with phyllo (see Basics) and working with 2 sheets for each roll, make 3 or 4 12-inch rolls. Place filling on short end of prepared phyllo, roll once, fold in edges and roll like jelly roll. Place seam side down on buttered baking sheet, brush rolls well with butter and bake in a 350° oven until golden. Remove to serving board and cool 10 minutes. Slice on diagonal into 1-inch slices. Serve immediately.
Makes 3 to 4 dozen slices

THE FERTILE CRESCENT

SYRIAN SILK-WORM COCOONS

SYRIAN LENTIL SOUP

Bring to boil:
**1-1/2 cups brown lentils, well
washed
6 cups lamb stock
1-1/2 teaspoons salt
2 tablespoons lemon juice
1/4 teaspoon each cumin and
black pepper**
Lower heat, cover and cook
gently 15 minutes. Add and
bring back to boil:
1/2 cup long-grain rice
Cover and simmer 15 minutes.
Add and bring back to boil:
**more stock to keep same level
3 cups shredded cabbage or
spinach**
Cover and simmer 5 minutes.
Sauté, stirring often, until soft in:
**3 tablespoons butter
1 onion, sliced into rings
1 teaspoon paprika
1/4 teaspoon cumin**
Add onions to soup. Just before
serving adjust seasonings and add:
lemon juice to taste
Serves 4 to 6

LEBANESE
SHURBAT ALKIBBI
(Soup with Kibbeh Balls)

Prepare:
**1/2 recipe basic kibbeh
  (page 78)**
Form into about 48 small balls
and refrigerate 1 hour. In heavy
skillet heat:
3 tablespoons butter
Brown kibbeh balls on all sides
a portion at a time so they do not
touch in skillet, adding more
butter if needed. Remove and set
aside. In browning skillet sauté
until golden, adding butter if
needed:
1-1/2 cups minced onion
1 garlic clove, minced (optional)
2/3 cup long-grain rice
Add and stir well:
2 quarts chicken broth
1 2-inch stick cinnamon
1 teaspoon salt
1/2 teaspoon black pepper
1/4 teaspoon allspice
Bring to boil and cook 10 minutes. Add:
kibbeh balls
Cook another 10 minutes or
until rice is tender. Remove
cinnamon stick and adjust seasonings. Just before serving stir in:
2/3 cup minced parsley
Serves 6 to 8

LEBANESE
CHILLED MELON SOUP

Halve lengthwise:
1 large cantaloupe
Remove seeds and with melon
scoop, carefully form 8 to 12
thin curls for garnish. Remove
remaining meat and chop. In
saucepan combine chopped
cantaloupe with:
1 pint half-and-half
**1 small chicken breast, boiled,
  skinned, boned and minced**
2 tablespoons sugar
**1/4 teaspoon each salt and
  cinnamon**
Bring to gentle boil, lower heat
and simmer 10 minutes. Cool and
purée in blender. Dissolve:
3 tablespoons cornstarch, in
1/2 pint half-and-half
Add to purée and cook and
stir until slightly thickened.
Add:
1 cup Mandorcrema*
Cook and stir until slightly
thickened, adding milk if
needed. Chill thoroughly and
adjust seasonings.
Serve topped with:
reserved curls of melon
dollops of yoghurt
Serves 4 to 6
*Middle Eastern almond wine

SYRIAN
KISHIK SOUP

Gently sauté until soft in:
1/3 cup olive oil
1 cup minced onions
Stir in:
1 cup kishik*
Cook and stir 1 minute. Gradually stir in until smooth and
thickened:
3-1/2 to 4 cups chicken broth
**salt, pepper and powdered cloves
  to taste**
When heated and ready to serve
sprinkle with:
**2 hard-cooked eggs, finely
  chopped**
1/4 cup finely minced parsley
Serve with:
lemon wedges
Serves 4
*Kishik, a mixture of ground
  wheat, spices and laban (yoghurt)
  dried in the sun and sieved to dry
  powder, is available in Middle
  Eastern stores. It has an unusual
  flavor for those who want to
  experiment.

THE FERTILE CRESCENT

LIEUT. COL. T. E. LAWRENCE
IN DAMASCUS OCT. 1, 1918

LEBANESE CAULIFLOWER WITH AVOCADO TARATOUR

Boil until tender in:
1 tablespoon lemon juice
boiling water to cover
1 large head cauliflower
Drain and place on bed of:
curly endive
Drizzle with:
avocado taratour sauce
   (following)
Sprinkle with:
toasted sesame seeds
Serve hot or chilled with meat
or fish. Excellent for a cold buffet.
Serves 8

AVOCADO TARATOUR

Combine and blend until smooth:
1 large ripe avocado, mashed
1 cup tahini dressing (see Basics)

LEBANESE TABBULI
(Bulghur Salad)

This salad is claimed by both the Lebanese and Syrians, as are most foods in their cuisines. One may say they are twin cuisines. A few variations exist, depending on one's taste for certain salad ingredients. You may also add your choice of avocados, etc., as long as you stay with the basic recipe in order to fully enjoy this different salad.

Soak in cold water to cover
1 hour:
1 cup fine bulghur, well washed
Drain and place on cloth napkin or cheesecloth and squeeze out moisture. Mix with:
2 cups finely chopped parsley
Toss with:
1/2 cup finely chopped green onions
1/2 cup or more chopped fresh mint
1/4 cup lemon juice
1 teaspoon allspice
1/2 teaspoon salt
1/4 teaspoon black pepper
Adjust seasonings and refrigerate. Wash and separate leaves of:
1 head romaine lettuce

Dry, wrap in towel and refrigerate. Just before serving, toss into bulghur mixture:
1/4 cup olive oil
3 ripe tomatoes, peeled and finely chopped
Place some of the romaine leaves on a serving platter and mound bulghur mixture on top. Surround with remaining leaves which guests should use to scoop up the tabbuli.
Garnish with:
lemon and tomato wedges
Serves 6 to 8

LEBANESE BABA GHANNOUJ
(Eggplant Salad)

Hold over open flame until skin is crispy and eggplant tender to the touch:
1 large eggplant
Remove skin and place pulp in colander to drain for a few minutes. Place pulp in a wooden bowl and chop. Then combine:
2 to 3 tablespoons tahini*, mixed with
2 tablespoons water
1/4 cup or more lemon juice
1 or 2 garlic cloves, mashed
1/2 teaspoon salt

Stir into eggplant and adjust seasonings. Place on serving plate and sprinkle with:
1 tablespoon olive oil
pomegranate seeds (optional)
finely chopped parsley
Serves 4
*Sesame seed paste available in Middle Eastern markets.

SYRIAN EGGPLANT SALAD

Hold over open flame until skin is crispy and eggplant tender to the touch:
1 large eggplant
Remove skin, place pulp in colander to drain and dice the eggplant. Rub bowl with cut garlic and place eggplant in bowl with:
1 onion, grated
3 tablespoons minced parsley
2 tablespoons minced fresh mint
2 tablespoons vinegar
1/4 cup olive oil
salt and pepper to taste
Just before serving toss in:
2 ripe tomatoes, cut in eighths
Serve chilled with garnish of:
fresh mint sprigs
Serves 4

THE FERTILE CRESCENT

KIBBEH BIS-SAYNIYYI
(Baked Kibbeh)

Kibbeh is the national dish of both Lebanon and Syria. The secret is to pound the mixture so well that it forms a paste. A laborious feat to achieve the desired texture and taste is involved. The traditional method is simple enough but the execution requires "blessed hands." To save time and energy, a meat grinder using the fine blade will result in the success of a kibbeh to earn the approval of the most skeptical Lebanese or Syrian! To win the first round, your butcher is involved. Have him bone a small leg of lamb with a little fat, cube and grind it twice. Then proceed with the recipe.

Soak 10 minutes in cold water to cover:

2 cups fine bulghur

Drain and squeeze dry in cheesecloth. Combine with:

2 pounds leg of lamb with
   a little fat, ground twice
1 large onion, grated
1-1/2 teaspoons salt
1/2 teaspoon black pepper
1/4 teaspoon allspice

Grind twice more or knead, dipping hands frequently in cold water and adding water to the meat mixture if needed, 15 to 20 minutes until very smooth and elastic. Set aside and use as basic kibbeh.

Brown in:

4 tablespoons butter
1 cup pine nuts

Add and sauté 10 minutes:

1 pound ground lamb shoulder

Add and cook until onions are limp:

1 cup finely chopped onion
1/2 teaspoon each salt and
   cinnamon
1/4 teaspoon each allspice and
   black pepper

Remove from fire and add:

2 tablespoons chopped fresh mint

Adjust seasonings and set aside. Generously butter a 9x12-inch shallow baking pan. Press 1/3 basic kibbeh firmly into pan, cover with ground lamb filling and spread remaining kibbeh on top, pressing firmly and wetting hands with cold water. Slice through to make diamond shapes and press onto meat:

1/4 cup sesame seeds (optional)

Drizzle over all:

2 tablespoons each olive oil
   and melted butter

Bake in 400° oven 20 minutes, lower heat to 300° and bake 20 minutes longer or until golden. Serve cut into diamond shapes. Serves 8

KIBBEH NAYÉ

Prepare basic kibbeh in preceding recipe. Adjust seasonings and form on round plate into a large mound. Make a well in the center and indentations in a spoke pattern emanating from the well. Drizzle over mound:

3 tablespoons olive oil

Garnish with:

chopped green onions

Serves 2 dozen as appetizer

THE FERTILE CRESCENT

THE KEEPER OF MAHOMET'S FOOTPRINT

LEBANESE
LENTIL PILAF

Sauté until onions are tender in:
1/4 pound butter
1 cup finely chopped onions
2 tablespoons chopped parsley
1/2 teaspoon allspice
1 garlic clove, minced
Combine:
2 cups cooked lentils (see Basics)
1 cup pilaff (see Basics)
Toss onion mixture into lentil
mixture and serve.
Serves 4 to 6

SYRIAN
LENTILS AND NOODLES

Sauté until soft in:
4 tablespoons butter
1 large onion, minced
Add and stir well to mix:
2 cups cooked lentils (see Basics)
Toss in:
1/2 pound thin noodles, cooked
    and drained
salt and pepper to taste
Transfer to heated platter and
over all pour:
1/4 pound burnt butter
Serve as accompaniment for
meat or fowl dishes.
Serves 6

STUFFED CABBAGE

Cut center core from:
1 large cabbage
Put into large pot core side down.
Cover with:
boiling water
Bring back to boil and blanch
5 minutes. Remove and drain
in colander. When cool, separate
leaves, which should be soft but
not overcooked. Set aside.
Combine and mix well:
1 cup long-grain rice
1/2 cup minced onions
1 egg, beaten
2 tablespoons each minced parsley, olive oil and tomato sauce
1 garlic clove, minced
1 teaspoon each salt and minced mint
1/2 teaspoon each allspice and black pepper
Place a tablespoon or more stuffing mixture on core end of cabbage leaves. Roll once, fold in edges and roll like jelly roll. Place excess leaves on bottom of heavy saucepan. Place cabbage rolls seam side down, on leaves, placing rolls made from leaves closest to the core on the bottom. Sprinkle each layer with:
olive oil
beef or chicken broth
When pot is filled pour over cabbage rolls:
beef or chicken broth to cover
Weigh down with heavy plate, cover pot and cook over low heat approximately 1 hour or until leaves are tender and rice is done. Remove to platter and pour juices over.
Serves 6

SYRIAN
BATINJAN WIA JOBAN
(Eggplant Casserole)

Cut into 1/4-inch slices:
1 large eggplant
Salt lightly and let stand in colander 30 minutes. Pat dry.
Beat together:
2 eggs
1 teaspoon milk
1/2 teaspoon salt
1/4 teaspoon pepper
2 tablespoons grated Kefalotyri or Parmesan cheese
Dip eggplant slices in egg mixture and brown, adding more oil as needed, on both sides in:
1/4 cup olive oil
Remove and drain on paper toweling. Layer half the eggplant slices in shallow buttered 9x9-inch baking dish. Cover layer with:
sliced peeled tomatoes
thinly sliced Mozzarella cheese
minced parsley
Repeat layers, ending with an extra layer of tomatoes.
Drizzle over all and set aside:
1 tablespoon olive oil
Combine and beat well:
1 egg, beaten
3 ripe tomatoes, peeled and chopped
3 tablespoons each tomato paste and water
1/2 cup minced onions
1/2 teaspoon salt
1/4 teaspoon pepper
Pour over eggplant mixture and bake in 325° oven 20 minutes or until heated and bubbly.
Remove from oven, cool slightly and cut into squares.
A perfect brunch dish or accompaniment to meats or fowl.
Serves 6

THE FERTILE CRESCENT

SYRIAN
SAFFRON FISH CASSEROLE

Place in buttered shallow
baking pan:
2 halibut steaks approximately
　　1 inch thick
Sprinkle with:
3 tablespoons lemon juice
1/4 teaspoon salt
1/8 teaspoon pepper
3 tablespoons minced parsley
Dot with:
2 tablespoons butter
Broil at 250° for 20 minutes or
until fish flakes easily with fork.
When cool enough to handle,
carefully flake into slices, removing bones. Set aside.
Lightly brown in:
4 tablespoons butter
2 onions, slivered
Add and mix well:
1/2 teaspoon allspice
1/4 cup each pine nuts and
　　sultanas
2 tablespoons olive oil
2 cups pilaff with saffron
　　(see Basics)
1/4 cup lemon juice
2 tablespoons chopped parsley
salt and pepper to taste
Place half of mixture in buttered
casserole, top with half of
reserved fish and sprinkle with:
1 tablespoon lemon juice

Repeat layers. Gently brown in:
2 tablespoons each olive oil
　　and butter
2 tablespoons pine nuts
Pour over fish and sprinkle with:
2 tablespoons chopped fresh mint
Bake in 350° oven 15 minutes or
until heated through.
Serves 4

FISH FILLETS WITH TAHINI

Pat dry and sprinkle with:
salt and pepper
4 halibut or other firm white
　　fish fillets
Lightly brown fillets in:
2 tablespoons olive oil
Place each fillet on a square of
heavy foil and sprinkle over them:
juice of 2 lemons
1/4 cup minced parsley
3 garlic cloves, minced
1/4 cup minced blanched
　　almonds
2 tablespoons olive oil
Seal well and bake in 450° oven
20 minutes. Place fish in foil
on serving platter, open foil
and spoon over each fillet:
tahini dressing (see Basics)
Surround with:
small new cooked potatoes
lemon wedges
Serve with additional sauce.
Serves 4

LEBANESE
RABBIT WITH
LENTIL PILAF

Cut into pieces and pat dry:
1 rabbit, approximately 3 pounds
Coat pieces with:
flour seasoned with salt and
　　pepper
Sauté until tender in:
4 tablespoons butter
1 cup finely chopped onions
1 garlic clove, minced
Push aside and brown rabbit,
adding more butter if needed.
Sprinkle with:
1/2 teaspoon allspice
2 tablespoons minced parsley
Add:
1 cup chicken broth
Cover and cook over low heat,
basting often and adding water
as needed, 45 minutes or until
rabbit is tender. Add:
1/4 cup raisins
Remove from fire and let rest,
covered, 10 minutes. Arrange
rabbit on lentil pilaf (page 80)
and pour sauce over. Serve
with spinach salad.
Serves 4

SYRIAN SFEEHA
(Meat Tarts)

Prepare:
1 recipe anise bread (page 85)
While dough is rising, combine and blend well:
1 pound lean ground lamb or beef
1 large onion, grated
juice of 1 lemon
1/4 cup pine nuts lightly browned in
2 tablespoons butter
1 teaspoon salt
1/2 teaspoon allspice
1/4 teaspoon freshly ground black pepper
3 to 4 tablespoons yoghurt (optional)
After second rising of dough, flatten as directed and on each round spread a portion of the meat mixture. Bring edges up slightly and place on lightly oiled cookie sheets. Bake in 350° oven 15 to 20 minutes. Broil 2 or 3 minutes and serve immediately.
Makes 3 dozen

THE WHEEL OF AMIN DOBEICY OF JISR AL QADI

THE FERTILE CRESCENT

SYRIAN STUFFED APPLES

A regal accompaniment to festive fowl or roast dishes. As a dessert served chilled with its sauce, it is superb.

Cut in half crosswise:
4 very large green apples
Cut a thin layer from bottom of each half so it stands evenly. Carefully scoop out pulp, chop and reserve, leaving a 1/4-inch shell. Brush outside of shells lavishly with:
melted butter
Roll in:
shredded coconut
Press coconut into apple skin with fingers and place in buttered shallow baking pan. Set aside. To reserved apple pulp add:
4 fresh figs, peeled and chopped*
1 cup shredded coconut
3/4 cup chopped walnuts and blanched almonds
1/2 cup brown sugar
2 tablespoons granulated sugar
1/2 teaspoon rose water
1/4 teaspoon each nutmeg and cinnamon
8 whole cloves
water and/or fruit juice to cover

Bring to boil, lower heat and simmer until sauce is slightly thickened. With slotted spoon remove ingredients from pot and stuff apple halves. Place in center of each half:
1 fig, peeled and stuffed with
1 whole blanched almond
Spoon onto each stuffed half:
1 teaspoon of the syrup from pot
Sprinkle with:
shredded coconut
Carefully pour balance of syrup and ingredients around apples in baking pan, cover with foil and bake in 300° oven 25 to 30 minutes, or until apples are tender. Do not baste. Serve each apple hot or cold on a bed of the syrup.
Serves 8
*If using canned figs, drain and reserve juices. If using dried figs, cook until tender in water to cover with 3 tablespoons sugar. Reserve cooking water and use as you would canned juices.

SYRIAN STUFFED BREAST OF VEAL

Have butcher cut pocket in:
1 5-pound breast of veal
Sprinkle with:
2 tablespoons lemon juice
salt and pepper
Set aside while making stuffing. Soak 1 hour in water to cover:
1 cup bulghur
Sauté until onions are soft in:
1/3 cup butter
2 cups minced onion
1 teaspoon salt
1/2 teaspoon allspice
1/4 teaspoon each powdered ginger and black pepper
Drain bulghur and add to onions with:
1 cup cooked garbanzo beans (see Basics)
1/4 cup pine nuts
Mix well and adjust seasonings to taste. Stuff veal pocket. Place breast in baking pan. Cover with:
thinly sliced veal fat
Roast in 350° oven 1-1/2 hours until tender and nicely browned. Last half hour of cooking, bake any extra stuffing in buttered casserole.
Serves 6

SYRIAN
KA-ICK
(Anise Bread)

Combine in bowl and set aside:
4 cups flour
1/2 cup sugar
1/2 teaspoon salt
1/2 teaspoon anise seeds
1/4 teaspoon mahleb*
Melt in:
3/4 cup milk
1/4 pound butter
Cool to lukewarm and dissolve
in milk:
**1 yeast cake or 1 tablespoon
  dry yeast**
Make a well in the flour and pour
milk mixture into it. Add with
milk mixture:
**2 eggs at room temperature,
  beaten**
Mix well and turn out on floured
board. Knead well until smooth
and elastic. Cover with tea towel
and let stand 2 hours in a warm
place until almost doubled in size.
Form into 2 dozen circles approximately 3 inches in diameter.
Cover with slightly dampened
tea towel and let rise another
30 minutes. Flatten circles into
rounds approximately 1/2 inch
thick. Place on cookie sheet in
250° oven until bottoms are
golden. Broil to brown tops.

Combine, bring to boil and
remove from heat:
4 tablespoons butter
1/4 cup milk
1/2 cup sugar
1 tablespoon rose water
1/2 teaspoon anise seeds
Dip rounds in syrup to coat and
place on cookie sheets to cool.
Makes 2 dozen
*Ground Syrian spice available
in Middle Eastern stores.

SYRIAN
SESAME BAKLAVA

Baklava recipes are generally
standard except for variations
in the spices and nuts used. This
Syrian baklava is unique in its
use of sesame seeds.

Combine and mix well:
**3 to 4 cups coarsely ground
  blanched almonds**
**3/4 cup sesame seeds, browned in
4 tablespoons butter**
1/2 cup sugar
1 teaspoon grated lemon rind
1 tablespoon orange flower water
1/2 teaspoon cinnamon
1/4 teaspoon nutmeg

Follow directions for working
with phyllo (see Basics), using:
1 pound phyllo
**approximately 1 pound sweet
  butter**
One at a time, place 6 buttered
phyllo sheets into a buttered
9x12-inch baking pan. Sprinkle
with half of the nut mixture,
cover with 6 more buttered sheets
and sprinkle with remaining nut
mixture. Cover with remaining
buttered phyllo sheets. Smooth
top sheet well and tuck and fold
ends and sides in neatly. Brush
top lavishly with butter. With a
very sharp knife or razor blade,
cut into diamond shapes through
top layer. Bake in a 350° oven 45
minutes, or until delicately
browned. While baklava is baking,
bring to boil:
2 cups water
2 cups sugar
1/2 cup honey
**1 tablespoon each orange flower
  water and freshly squeezed
  lemon juice**
1/2 teaspoon allspice
Stir to dissolve sugar, lower fire
and simmer, stirring often, until
syrupy. When baklava is baked,
pour all but 1/3 cup of the syrup
over immediately and let cool.
Just before serving pour remaining syrup over.

ARMENIA

THE ARMENIAN cuisine is simpler than many others in the Middle East consisting of fewer sauces and of sweet, rather than hot spices. Yet the Armenians have exerted an influence on dining throughout the world far out of proportion to the position accorded them in recorded history. While credited with retaining their identity, unique language, strong national feeling, customs and churches in the face of incredible adversity, Armenians seem never to have inspired great swashes of color on the giant canvas historians like to paint. This I found incomprehensible, so I searched for a reason. The first thing I found was that they never stayed put on maps. Vague references to the "Armenian Nation" variously refer to Hittite peoples from Europe or Central Asia dominating the area from the Black to Caspian Seas and south to the Persian Gulf from 1900 to 1200 B.C., to Mt. Ararat where Noah's ark was stranded, to the first kingdom converted from Zoroastrianism to Christianity in 301 A.D., to a tiny country on the northeast corner of the Mediterranean in 1350, and to a modern republic of the U.S.S.R.

When I studied how the Armenians had been divided and scattered by Egyptians, Arabs, Mongols, Persians, Turks and Russians, I realized there's more to culture than geography. The story of their persecution by nomadic Kurds in 1893 and in 1915 by Turks who drove them from their homeland into the Iranian desert brought tears to my eyes, but I began to see the light.

The persecutors were the losers; the rest of the world gained. In New York, California, London or wherever refugee Armenian artists, dramatists, writers, musicians, architects, merchants or restaurateurs found freedom to express their irrepressible creativity they have brought a culture that refuses to be restricted geographically or politically. Archeologists and historians may have trouble defining Armenian contributions to civilization, but surely you and I will not, especially when it comes to fine food.

ARMENIA

TURSI
(Pickled Vegetables)

My friend Genevieve Megetanian Levon inherited her culinary knowledge from her grandfather, a renowned Armenian chef. This is her recipe for the favorite pickled vegetables dish of Armenia.

Prepare vegetables and set aside:
cauliflower, broken into small flowerets
celery, cut into pieces
cabbage, cut into wedges
carrots, cut into quarters
Sterilize wide-mouth quart jars with tight new lids. In each jar place:
1 garlic clove

Bring to boil:
3 quarts water
2 cups white vinegar
1 cup coarse non-iodized salt
6 to 8 dried hot red peppers, lightly crushed
2 teaspoons sugar
2 or 3 sprigs fresh dill
Boil 10 minutes. Pack vegetables tightly into jars and pour brine over. Seal jars and store 4 to 6 weeks before using.

TANABOUR
(Yoghurt Soup)

This is another of Genevieve Megetanian Levon's recipes.

Soak overnight in:
water to cover
1 cup barley
Drain and place in saucepan with:
3 cups water
1/2 teaspoon salt
1/4 teaspoon pepper
Bring to boil, lower heat, cover and cook, adding water as needed, until tender. Set aside. Sauté until browned in:
3 tablespoons butter
1 cup finely chopped onions

Set aside. In large saucepan over low heat put:
2 pints plain yoghurt
Break in and beat until well mixed:
1 egg
Add and beat well:
1 tablespoon flour
Blend in and cook and stir until soup comes to a boil:
4 cups chicken broth
Lower fire and add, stirring constantly:
reserved barley and onions
In small skillet sauté to wilt in:
4 tablespoons butter
1 cup chopped fresh coriander (substitute fresh parsley or mint)
Add coriander to soup and season to taste with:
salt and pepper
Stir well and serve hot.
Serves 6 to 8

GREAT ARARAT FROM SARDAR BULAKH VALLEY

VOSP
(Lentil Soup)

Bring to boil:
6 cups lamb broth
1/3 cup hulled barley, well washed (available in health food stores and some markets)
Lower heat, cover and simmer 1 hour. Add and bring back to boil:
1 cup brown lentils, well washed
3/4 cup minced parsley
Cover and cook 30 minutes or until lentils are tender but still firm. Sauté until soft in:
6 tablespoons butter
1 large onion, cut in rings
1 garlic clove, minced
1 teaspoon paprika
Add to soup last 5 minutes of cooking. Adjust seasonings with:
salt and pepper
Serve with sprinkling of:
minced fresh dill
Serves 4 to 6

ARMENIAN EGGPLANT SALAD

Hold over open flame until skin is crispy and eggplant tender to the touch:
1 large eggplant
Remove skin and place pulp in colander to drain for a few minutes. Then place pulp in wooden bowl and chop. Add to bowl:
1 large tomato, peeled and chopped
1 medium onion, grated
1/2 green pepper, finely minced
2/3 cup minced parsley
1 teaspoon salt
1/2 teaspoon cinnamon or dried mint
1 to 2 teaspoons vinegar
1 tablespoon or more olive oil
Blend well and adjust seasonings. Place on serving platter and garnish with:
thinly sliced green pepper rings
Serves 4

ARMENIA

MELON DOLMA

Dolma varieties are infinite. Unusual in taste and appearance is this melon dolma.

Soak 30 minutes or more:
1/2 cup raisins in
brandy to cover
Wash, dry and halve:
2 medium-large cantaloupes
Remove seeds and scoop out small melon balls, leaving a 1/4-inch shell. Set shells and melon balls aside.
Sauté gently in:
2 tablespoons butter
1 pound ground lean choice
**   lamb or beef**
1 onion, minced
Stir in:
1-1/2 cups steamed rice (see
**   Basics)**
reserved melon balls
1/2 cup pine nuts
reserved raisins and their brandy
1/2 cup wine
1/2 teaspoon salt
1/4 teaspoon pepper
1 teaspoon cinnamon or allspice
additional butter if needed

Cover and simmer over low heat 10 minutes. Remove from heat and fill melon shells, packing tightly. Sprinkle over top of each filled melon half:
bread crumbs
Wrap well in heavy foil and place in baking dish. Bake in 325° oven 40 minutes. Unwrap, discard foil and place on serving platter. Garnish with:
cooked peas
Pour over all:
1/4 cup pine nuts, browned in
1 tablespoon butter
Serves 4

ARMENIAN PILAFF

In skillet with tight-fitting lid melt:
1/4 pound butter
Add and stir until gently browned:
3/4 cup crushed fedia (coiled,
**   very thin vermicelli)**
Add and sauté 5 minutes, stirring:
1 cup long-grain rice
Stir in:
2 cups hot chicken broth
Cover, lower heat and cook 20 minutes. Remove from heat and let stand for 10 minutes. Fluff with fork and serve as accompaniment to meats and fowl.
Serves 4

BEAN PLAKI

Cook 30 minutes in water to cover:
2 cups northern beans, washed
Drain and set aside. Lightly brown in:
1/2 cup olive oil
2 onions, finely chopped
3/4 cup diced carrots
1/2 cup chopped celery
**   with leaves**
2 garlic cloves, minced
1/2 cup chopped parsley
1 crushed bay leaf
Add and stir well:
2 large ripe tomatoes, peeled
**   and chopped, or**
1 16-ounce can whole tomatoes,
**   drained and chopped**
water to cover (if using canned
**   tomatoes, include juices)**
Cover and simmer 25 minutes or until beans are tender. Ten minutes before end of cooking period, add and stir well:
2 tablespoons each olive oil
**   and vinegar**
Cool and chill. Serve on platter with garnish of:
olives
minced parsley
Serves 4 to 6

TOMB AT
AKHLAT

ARMENIA

STUFFED TOMATOES

Cut 1/2-inch tops off:
4 very large tomatoes
Carefully scoop out pulp, leaving
a 1/2-inch shell. Drain and
sprinkle inside of shell with salt,
pepper and a little sugar. Set
aside. Chop half the pulp and
set aside. Reserve remaining pulp
for another use. Sauté until
onion is transparent in:
2 tablespoons olive oil
1 cup minced onion
1/4 cup minced parsley
**1/2 teaspoon each salt, sugar and
　　allspice**
1/4 teaspoon black pepper
1 tablespoon chopped fresh basil
Add reserved chopped tomato
pulp and:
1 cup cooked lentils (see Basics)
1 cup fine bulghur
Sauté, stirring often, 10 minutes.
Adjust seasonings to taste and
stuff tomato shells. Brush outside
of shells with:
olive oil
Sprinkle over top of tomatoes:
1/4 cup chopped walnuts
1 tablespoon olive oil
Press tops gently, place in shallow baking pan and bake in 350°
oven 20 minutes or until tender.
Serve hot or room temperature.
Serves 4

ARMENIA

STUFFED ZUCCHINI

Halve crosswise and then lengthwise:

2 large zucchini (approximately 12 ounces each)

Scoop out pulp, leaving a shell approximately 3/4-inch thick. Chop pulp and reserve. Parboil shells 2 to 3 minutes in boiling salted water. Drain, dry, sprinkle with salt and pepper and set aside. Sauté until onions are transparent in:

3 tablespoons olive oil
1-1/2 cups minced onion
1 clove garlic, minced
reserved chopped pulp
1/2 teaspoon each allspice and salt
1/4 teaspoon black pepper

Add and sauté 10 minutes, stirring:

1 cup cooked lentils (see Basics)
1 cup bulghur

Adjust seasonings and stuff into shells. Brush outside of shells with:

olive oil

Sprinkle with:

chopped walnuts
olive oil

Press down gently, cover and bake in 350° oven 20 minutes. Serve hot or room temperature. Serves 8

KURDISH CHIEFTAIN ARMED WITH DIRK CIRCA 1897

TORLU TAVA
(Vegetable Casserole)

Torlu is a mixed vegetable casserole made throughout the Middle East with a variety of herbs and vegetables. Any combination of vegetables may be used, according to availability.

Prepare vegetables and set aside:
1 large or 2 small eggplants, cut in 1/2-inch slices
4 small zucchini, sliced
3 carrots, sliced lengthwise
3 large onions, sliced
1 pound fresh or frozen okra
1 large green pepper, cut in julienne
4 large ripe tomatoes, sliced

Have ready:
1 cup minced parsley
1/4 cup chopped fresh mint
3 garlic cloves, minced
2 tablespoons chopped fresh basil (optional)
1/2 to 3/4 cup olive oil or as needed
salt and pepper
Brush a shallow baking pan with olive oil and layer vegetables in any order, sprinkling each layer with the seasonings and oil. End with a layer of tomatoes. Cover and bake in a 350° oven approximately 45 minutes. Test for tenderness before removing from oven.
Serves 8

HERISAH

Soak overnight in water to cover:
1-1/2 cups medium bulghur
Drain and set aside.
Boil until tender in water to cover:
1 2- to 3-pound chicken
1 teaspoon salt
1/2 teaspoon black pepper
Remove chicken, reserve stock and skin and bone chicken. Shred meat finely and combine in saucepan with:

drained bulghur
reserved stock to cover
Bring to boil, lower heat and cook, beating almost constantly and adding stock as needed, until mixture is smooth and mushy. Continue this process 1 hour, or put mixture through meat grinder to crush and combine it. The herisah should be the consistency of oatmeal. Adjust seasonings with salt and pepper and place on heated serving platter. Melt until browned:
1/4 pound butter
1/2 teaspoon each paprika and cumin
Pour over herisah and serve immediately.
Serves 4 to 6

ARMENIA

KOUZOU KZARTMA
(Lamb Shanks with Lentil and Bulghur Pilaff)

Cut into cubes and set aside:
1 large unpeeled eggplant
Rub well into:
4 medium lamb shanks, cracked
salt
paprika
minced garlic
Brown on all sides in:
3 to 4 tablespoons olive oil
Remove to roasting pan and
pour over:
4 large ripe tomatoes, peeled and
   chopped
1 8-ounce can tomato sauce
1 cup minced onions
half the reserved eggplant
1 cup each white wine and water
Mix well and sprinkle with:
2 teaspoons dried basil, or
5 teaspoons minced fresh basil
Cover and bake in 350° oven
1 hour or until shanks are
tender, basting several times,
adding equal amounts of wine
and water to keep sauce approximately 1 inch deep in pan. Remove from oven and keep warm.

In skillet fry until tender and
golden brown in:
5 tablespoons butter
remaining eggplant cubes
Remove lamb shanks to large
heated serving platter and pour
pan juices over. Surround with
fried eggplant cubes and serve
with lentil and bulghur pilaff.
Serves 4

LENTIL AND BULGHUR PILAFF

Brown in:
6 tablespoons butter
1 cup minced onions
Add and mix well:
2 cups cooked lentils (see Basics)
1 cup cooked fine bulghur
   (see Basics)
1/4 cup minced parsley
1/2 teaspoon allspice
salt and pepper to taste
Simmer, stirring constantly,
5 minutes. Mound on heated
serving platter and pour over:
1/2 cup pine nuts, browned in
6 tablespoons butter

TASS KEBAB
(Lamb Kebab Stew)

In large heavy skillet, sauté until
gently browned in:
4 tablespoons butter
2 pounds boneless lamb, cubed
1 cup minced onions
2 garlic cloves, minced
Season with:
1/2 teaspoon salt
1/4 teaspoon pepper
1/2 teaspoon each nutmeg, allspice, cumin and paprika
Add and stir well:
1/2 cup white wine
1 8-ounce can tomato sauce
1/4 cup minced parsley
Stir well to combine all ingredients and surround with:
1 pound small pearl onions
Pour over lamb:
1/2 cup white wine
Cover and simmer about 45 minutes or until lamb is tender,
adding water if needed. Adjust
seasonings to taste. Remove from
fire and serve with:
hunker begendi (following)
garnishing as directed.
Serves 6 to 8

HUNKER BEGENDI
(Eggplant Platter)

Broil, turning often, until skins
are blackened and pulp tender
to the touch of a fork:
2 large eggplants
Peel and put pulp in colander
to drain, patting gently to release
moisture. Place in deep bowl,
mash and whip until the consistency of mashed potatoes.
Add and continue to whip:
1 cup Béchamel sauce (see Basics)
salt and pepper to taste
Mound on heated platter and
make a well in center. Over
eggplant pour:
1/4 cup pine nuts heated until
golden brown in
2 tablespoons butter
Fill with tass kebab (preceding). Sprinkle with:
minced parsley
Garnish platter with:
green pepper rings
lemon wedges
Serves 6 to 8
Variation
Serve eggplant platter separately
to accompany other entrées such
as shish kebabs.

THE NORTH WALL OF THE CHURCH AT AKHTAMAR

FIVE GENERATIONS 1894

HARPUT KUFTA
(Stuffed Meatballs)

Florence Yacoubian Vaty, of the famed and talented Yacoubian family, is a well-known concert pianist who is equally well known for her cuisine. Her recipe for Harput kufta, named after the Armenian city of Harput where it originated, is reputed to have the touch of her magic fingers. The choice of meat for this dish is identical to the Syrian and Lebanese kibbeh; a good cut of lamb with some fat, ground twice, is of utmost importance to the making of a light and succulent meatball. Have your butcher bone a small leg of lamb. Reserve the bones for stock and grind the meat twice. Use 2 pounds for the kufta and 2 pounds for the filling.

FIVE GENERATIONS

The little fellow pictured here is 80 years old. The woman on the left is his mother. The woman on the right is her mother. She, in turn, is the daughter of the lady seated next to the tyke's present cuddler, who is, needless to say, her own mother.

Filling
Lightly brown in:
2 tablespoons butter
2 pounds leg of lamb with some fat, ground twice
Add and sauté 25 minutes:
4 large onions, chopped
1 cup finely chopped green pepper
1/2 cup minced parsley
1 teaspoon each minced fresh mint, allspice and dried basil
1-1/2 teaspoons salt
1/2 teaspoon black pepper
Remove from heat and mix in:
1/4 cup chopped walnuts
Cool and chill several hours or overnight.

Meatballs (Kufta)
Soak 10 minutes in cold water to cover:
2 cups fine bulghur
Drain and combine with:
2 pounds leg of lamb, ground twice
2 medium onions, minced or grated
2 tablespoons finely minced parsley
1-1/2 teaspoons salt
1/2 teaspoon black pepper
Mix well and knead until smooth, wetting hands in cold water occasionally, for approximately 20 minutes. Set aside. Form filling mixture into 3/4-inch balls and set aside. Wet hands in ice water and take a walnut-size amount of kufta mixture and form a smooth ball. Make an indentation with forefinger, pressing and turning to make a wall of kufta. The thinner the wall, the lighter the stuffed kufta will be. Place one filling ball into the kufta shell, seal the opening, wet hands and smooth well, patting gently into slightly flattened round. Drop a dozen or so balls at a time into:
boiling lamb or beef stock
Lower heat and simmer 15 minutes or until balls rise to surface. Remove with slotted spoon and keep warm while cooking remaining meatballs. Serve hot with:
yoghurt
Or serve in a bowl with the broth.
Variations
In the filling substitute chopped pine nuts for walnuts; add with onions 1 cup minced peeled eggplant, or serve raw, formed into small balls for appetizer (meze); or form into a small sausage. Make a hole in center the length of the sausage with index finger and broil quickly.
Makes 60 balls

ARMENIA

CHEOREG

Combine and set aside:
**1 cup chopped blanched almonds
and/or walnuts**
1 cup sultanas
3 tablespoons brown sugar
1 teaspoon allspice
Sift into bowl:
4 cups flour
4 teaspoons baking powder
1/2 teaspoon salt
Heat:
1/2 cup milk
1/4 pound butter
Stir to melt butter. Cool slightly.
Make a well in center of flour
and pour in milk. Stir well and
blend in:
3 eggs, beaten with
3 tablespoons sugar
Mix well and turn out on floured
board. Using flour as needed and
moistening hands with melted
butter, knead until dough is soft
and smooth. Cut dough into 3
balls and roll each into a strip
3 inches wide and 14 inches long.

Brush each strip lavishly with:
melted butter
Sprinkle each strip with:
reserved nut mixture
Fold over in half lengthwise and
seal end. Curve to make a pin-
wheel, brush with:
beaten egg yolk
Sprinkle each wheel with mixture of:
3 tablespoons sugar
**1/4 cup finely chopped blanched
almonds and/or walnuts**
1 teaspoon allspice
Bake in 350° oven until golden,
approximately 40 minutes.
Makes 3 loaves

LOVASH BREAD

Dissolve in:
1/4 cup warm water
**1 yeast cake or 1 tablespoon
dry yeast**
Into mixing bowl sift:
approximately 5 cups flour
2 teaspoons salt

Make a well in center and pour
in:
dissolved yeast
2 cups warm milk
1 tablespoon sugar
1/4 pound butter, melted
Mix well, turn out on floured
board and knead until elastic and
smooth, adding more flour as
needed. Place dough in bowl
which has been brushed with
melted butter, turn to coat
dough, cover with tea towel and
let rise 3 hours. Divide dough into
4 parts. Keeping remaining dough
in bowl, roll one portion at a
time into a very thin oval or
round. Place on large ungreased
cookie sheet or 14-inch pizza pan
and bake on lowest rack of a preheated 350° oven 25 minutes or
until lightly browned and crisp.
Cool, stack and store in dry
place up to 2 weeks. Traditionally, the bread discs are sprinkled
lightly with cold water to soften
before serving. They may be
served without dampening,
broken and used for dipping into
various dishes.
Makes 4 discs

ARMENIAN DERVISH, 1893

ARMENIA

MUHALLEBI
(Quince Pudding)

Heat to dissolve sugar:
2 cups milk
1/4 cup sugar
Bring milk to boil, lower heat
and add, stirring constantly:
**2 tablespoons cornstarch,
   dissolved in**
3/4 cup water
1 teaspoon vanilla extract
3 tablespoons quince preserves*
**3 teaspoons minced blanched
   almonds**
Blend well and cook, stirring,
until thickened. Remove from
heat and pour into individual
glass dessert dishes. Sprinkle with:
cinnamon
chopped blanched almonds
Garnish with:
rose petals
Chill thoroughly before serving.
Serves 6 to 8
*Quince preserves may be pur-
chased in Middle Eastern stores.

ARMENIAN DERVISH

*This fellow inspired a religious
riot in Armenia circa the turn of
the century, which mayhem
resulted in the demise of about
500 people.*

99

MUSICIANS AT A WEDDING IN ALEXANDROPOL

ARMENIA

KADAIFF
(Also Kannaffe, Kadayif)

Combine and set aside:
2 cups coarsely ground pistachios and walnuts in any combination or proportions
1/2 cup sugar
1/2 teaspoon each allspice and nutmeg
Combine to separate strands and coat thoroughly:
1 pound kadaiff*
1/2 pound melted sweet butter
Pat half the kadaiff firmly into a buttered 10x14-inch shallow baking pan. Pour over:
1/4 pound melted sweet butter
Spread with:
reserved nut mixture
Cover with remaining kadaiff, pressing down gently. Pour over all:
1/2 cup melted sweet butter

With sharp knife cut into diamond shapes. Bake in 350° oven 45 minutes or until top is crisp and browned. While kadaiff is baking bring to boil:
2 cups sugar
2 cups water
2 tablespoons orange flower water
1 tablespoon freshly squeezed lemon juice
Stir to dissolve sugar and stirring often, simmer until syrupy. Add and set aside:
2 tablespoons almond liqueur
Remove kadaiff from oven and immediately pour all but 1/3 cup of the syrup evenly over. Cool. Just before serving pour rest of syrup over and serve with:
whipped cream
*Available in 1-pound packages at Middle Eastern and Greek specialty shops, usually frozen. Defrost in refrigerator overnight.

KHOHSHAB
(Fruit Compote)

Combine in saucepan:
1 cup sultanas
1 cup dried prunes
1 cup dried apricots
1 cup dried peaches
1/2 cup pomegranate juice
water to cover
3 tablespoons honey
1 2-inch stick cinnamon
1/4 teaspoon allspice
Bring to gentle boil and simmer until fruits are tender and liquid is syrupy. Chill well and spoon into chilled compote glasses. Sprinkle with:
chopped walnuts
Fresh fruits may be substituted for some of the dried. If using fresh, add them to the dried fruits after cooking.
Serves 8

MURRAH BEDOUIN IN THE EMPTY QUARTER SEARCHING FOR GRASS

NORTH OF THE SAHARA

"Pleasantest of all ties is the tie of host and guest."
—The Choephoroe

SHARING FOOD and drink with strangers was a duty as well as a pleasure and pastime to the simple, close-knit Semitic tribes of the Arabian peninsula roaming with their camels, goats and sheep in search of water and fodder perhaps as long ago as 3000 B.C. To each wanderer every other wanderer was a brother in the harsh struggle to survive. It was unthinkable to refuse sustenance to a guest, though it might mean slaughtering the last sheep. Equally unthinkable was that a guest might refuse such hospitality. Even an enemy who had broken his host's bread and eaten his salt could claim sanctuary for a day or so.

Tents were woven of goat hair; rugs from camel hair; clothing from sheep's wool. All three animals furnished meat, milk and cheese to add protein to a diet of barley, millet and dates. But wealth was measured mainly in terms of camels, those "ships of the desert" that carried an internal reserve of food and water in the fat of their humps, in addition to passengers and baggage on their backs.

These people had little art, architecture or written history of their own, yet one of them who became known as Mohammed ("messenger") triggered the building of an empire unparalleled in history based on religious conversion and political conquest. He laid no claim to his own immortality, merely new insight through divine revelation as to the nature of the one true God of his Hebrew ancestors, the Prophets. They had long ago discarded multiple angry gods of whimsy for a single Supreme Being. This God expressed compassion toward all people striving for a better life on earth and willing to follow precepts that would assure a return to Paradise in the hereafter.

NORTH OF THE SAHARA

Armed with the new religion of Islam ("submission"), fierce Arab wanderers literally burst out of their homeland in a *jihad,* or holy war. Within 100 years the Moslems ("those who submit") had conquered lands from the borders of Asia Minor and India to the Atlantic and into Spain and southern France. Islam itself, as a religion and a culture, spread even further. It is credited with fathering the Renaissance in Europe and influencing the arts, sciences and architecture throughout the world.

I can't help but be excited about what these people felt as Islam was accepted by other peoples who had tired of petty gods, as they wrested control from ruler after ruler of lands richer than their own. But even more exciting than their zealotry in religion and politics was the Arabs' insatiable appetite for culture in every form. They reveled in the wonders of new worlds where homes were more than tents, temples and tombs were spectacular edifices, and feelings were expressed in works of art and history in written words. They absorbed, preserved, expanded and spread the best of many ancient civilizations during a period when less astute warriors merely pillaged and destroyed.

Some say no great cuisine has ever been developed without several essential elements: an abundance of fine ingredients, a variety of cultural influences, a history including domination and a place in the sun, borrowings from imperialistic adventures, and a palace life of luxury with creative chefs in great kitchens.

Lush fields of grain, vegetables and fruits greeted Arab conquerors in the Nile delta and along other rivers and seacoasts, providing a welter of new ingredients. They found a place in the sun until expelled from Spain in the west and defeated by the Turks in the east in the late 1400's. And though common soldiers subsisted on traditional desert fare, Arab generals and rulers quickly recognized the pleasures of the palace foods of Egypt, Syria and Persia. Their drive to northwestern Africa brought them in contact with another great people in the Maghreb (now Morocco, Algeria, Tunisia and Libya). The Berbers, Hamites with probably a Nordic strain, adopted Islam without relinquishing their folk music, poetry or traditional foods. Some early Arabs and Berbers did intermarry, however, leading to the famous Moors of Morocco and Spain whose architecture is world renowned. Berber folklore attributes the ability of peasants to exist on minuscule amounts of grain to a mysterious personal power to multiply food called *kimia*—a kind of mind over matter. Yet the *diffa* (banquet), like the Bedouin *mansat* (feast of boiled lamb and rice), did more to turn their warlike leaders into refined monarchs.

Today the Arabic cuisine is as difficult to delineate and define as the hundreds of offshoots of the original Moslem religion, adopted by so many varied peoples but developed in many individualistic ways. Restaurants often fail to capture the feeling and flavor of Arabic dining, for commercial necessity has restricted the amazing variety and abundance of foods prepared by so many good home cooks who may speak Arabic, but whose ancestry may be as diverse as their foods. Arab hospitality features *shaban,* or total satisfaction, with abundance as an end in itself. *Diffas* of the Moroccans may comprise as many as 30 meat and poultry dishes, 12 salads and 32 sweetmeats. It is not expected that each of the many platters will be licked clean before being whisked away and replaced with another, for many a hungry mouth awaits behind the scene.

104

According to Berber folklore, it *is* important how one attacks such an embarrassment of culinary riches. Fingers (of the right hand only), washed at the table, should first enjoy each food, either by direct contact or with the aid of a piece of bread. Forks or spoons are rarely entrusted with the job of transporting any food, no matter how oily or moist, from dish to mouth. The thumb and first two fingers are considered to be in accord with the Prophet. One finger used alone signifies hatred; thumb and first finger, pride; thumb and three fingers, gluttony.

In the Arab language of food not only are ancient traditions of preparing, serving and eating preserved, but also the menu and dishes themselves, expanded, sometimes, with new ingredients. To the *mansat* of pre-Moslem times, the Bedouin dinner of rice and lamb and *shrak,* a whole-wheat crust baked over a campfire on a cast-iron dome, has been added demitasses of black, fresh-roasted coffee, ground and brought to a surging boil, then decanted to a second pot where cloves, cardamom seeds or other spices are added. The breads and cakes of old Egypt still persist in cosmopolitan Cairo and especially among the *fellaheen,* poor farmers with few alternative foods. *Feta,* a dish of bread, rice, meat and garlic, *fool,* slow-baked or long-simmered, seasoned beans, and *tamiya,* mashed deep-fried patties of fava beans with garlic, onions, coriander, parsley and cayenne are not limited to any single social stratum. *Gambari,* or prawns of the Red Sea, are a delicacy, as are baby pigeons and *esh es seraya,* "bread of the palace" soaked in syrup, baked and crowned with *eishta,* coagulate of rich milk. In Egypt, the couscous of the Maghreb is sometimes turned into a dessert by adding sweetening and nuts.

The Arab westward expansion brought interesting new Berber foods back to the East, but purists claim only in cities like Tunis, Algiers and Marrakech can one find the exquisite dishes based on humble Berber fare embellished with Arab, Egyptian, Persian, Spanish and French ideas. *Couscous,* the national dish of the Maghreb, essentially cracked wheat or wheat flour rolled into granules steamed over broth of chicken or lamb and vegetables, can be dull or delicious, depending on ingredients, spices and seasonings. *Bisteeya* was a humble dish of pigeon or chicken, eggs and sweetened almonds until glorified with thin flaky Persian pastry, lemon, onion sauce and cinnamon. *Mechoui,* roast lamb on a spit, pre-rubbed with garlic and ground cumin, must be cooked to perfection—crisp on the outside, tender enough inside to be eaten with the fingers. A *tagine* (stew) is not simply tossed together, but mysteriously concocted by a loving cook, just as is *djej emshmel,* a slowly simmered chicken, with just the right contrast of herbs, spices, olive and lemon. No wonder that restaurant chefs, unassured of "guests of Allah" at every meal, often fail to meet standards set by dedicated hosts preparing for special guests in more intimate home surroundings.

Old Moslem food restrictions like the nomad rejection of pork, the Judaistic abhorrence of bloods as a pollution, and prohibitions against alcohol in any form (possibly promulgated to prevent Islamic soldiers from getting drunk on the eve of battle) are not always followed to the letter. In fact, among my friends of Moslem heritage I find a number who recommend the use of wines and liqueurs in cooking, as well as for sipping separately to enhance the enjoyment of Middle Eastern foods.

NORTH OF THE SAHARA

I cannot resist a personal comment about the antagonisms that persist in the Middle East in spite of common historical bonds, similar religious concepts, and, on an individual basis, an almost reverent approach to hospitality. Rulers here have often massacred, enslaved or driven out minorities who threaten their existence or luxury, but in this they are not too different from the rest of the world. I respect men like Ibn Saud who felt strong measures were needed to unify his warlike Arab brothers. I feel a great affinity for the fabulous T. E. Lawrence, an outsider who fought to restore independence to proud Arab peoples dominated by the Turks for centuries.

I know when fiercely individualistic peoples struggle for existence in a harsh land there are bound to be conflicts, yet I would pray they would struggle together to fight hunger, disease and ignorance, not destroy each other.

If diversity and conflict must persist, I suggest it should be in the kitchen, not on the battlefield. Everywhere I read of Middle Eastern people vying for recognition as the very best hosts serving the very best foods. Oh, that such a feeling of friendly rivalry at the dinner table could be extended to the conference tables of diplomats!

Can Jews who say *shalom aleichem* (peace to you) be far removed from Arabs who express the same sentiment with *as-salaam' aleikum?*

EGYPTIAN ASSORTED DEEP FRIED VEGETABLES WITH EGG LEMON SAUCE

Parboil in salted water until barely tender:
cauliflowerets
Trim, quarter, remove choke and parboil in salted water until barely tender:
small artichokes
Slice lengthwise into strips:
zucchini and eggplant
Dip prepared vegetables into:
beaten egg
and then into:
flour

Deep fry vegetables until golden in:
hot corn or peanut oil
Drain on paper toweling and serve immediately with egg lemon sauce.

EGG LEMON SAUCE

Combine and heat until slightly thickened:
1 tablespoon cornstarch dissolved in
2 tablespoons water
1 cup chicken broth or stock
Keep hot.

Beat until stiff:
3 egg whites
Continue beating whites and add:
3 egg yolks
Beating constantly, gradually add:
6 tablespoons fresh lemon juice
Beating constantly until smooth and creamy gradually add:
hot thickened chicken broth
Makes 2 cups

INSCRIPTION FROM BILLBOARD IN CAIRO

"Drink Coca-Cola"

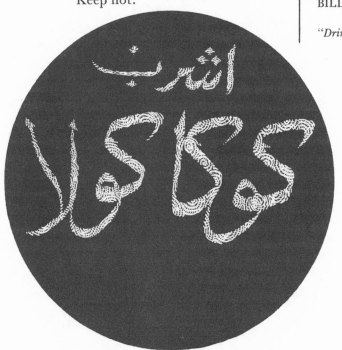

NORTH OF THE SAHARA

EGYPTIAN CHICKEN LIVER BREAD LOAF

I am addicted to home-baked bread but since I discovered a new product, frozen demi-loaves boxed and baked in the box and available frozen in all markets, I have used them in endless variations. This recipe was given to me by Paul Franks. Born in Cairo, he brought his early culinary training from Egypt to the United States and is now in Las Vegas where he is known as the "Egyptian gourmet."

Follow directions on 1 package:
"Bake-in-the-Box" Bread (ready dough)
When risen, brush with:
egg yolk, beaten
Sprinkle lavishly with:
sesame seeds
Bake as directed, cool and cut a 3/4-inch slice off top of loaf. Set aside. Carefully remove insides of loaf, leaving a 1/2-inch shell. Pull apart the inside bread into small pieces and set aside.

Sauté until tender in:
3 tablespoons butter
1/2 pound chicken livers, halved
Do not overcook. Reserve pan juices and chop livers. Put in blender with:
reserved juices
reserved bread
1 tablespoon minced parsley
1/2 teaspoon allspice
1 tablespoon orange juice
1/2 tablespoon rose water
salt and pepper to taste
Blend into a fine paste and remove from blender. Butter the inside shell of the bread lavishly with:
butter, softened
Pack half the liver pâté firmly into loaf and down the middle make a row of:
1/3 cup chopped fresh pistachio nuts
Pack remaining pâté in firmly, butter underside of top of bread and replace on loaf, pressing firmly to reform loaf. Wrap well in foil and chill. To serve, slice 1/4 inch thick, arrange slices on serving board and garnish with:
parsley sprigs
Greek olives
Makes approximately 24 slices

EGYPTIAN SHRIMP PÂTÉ

This is a variation of bread stuffed with chicken liver pâté. Prawns abound in Egypt. Paul Franks' recipe for this pâté, served in—of all places—Las Vegas, is a connoisseur's delight.

Following the same procedure for chicken liver bread loaf (preceding), prepare demi-loaf for stuffing.
Purée in blender:
1/2 pound cooked prawns or shrimp meat, or
2 4-1/2-ounce cans broken shrimp, drained
1/4 cup chopped toasted blanched almonds
1 tablespoon grated candied ginger
1/4 to 1/2 teaspoon curry powder
1 garlic clove, mashed
1 tablespoon fresh lemon juice
2 tablespoons finely chopped parsley
2 tablespoons melted butter
4 Kalamata (Greek) olives, chopped
reserved bread
salt and freshly ground black pepper to taste

Blend into smooth paste and follow directions for stuffing and serving bread loaf.
Variation
This pâté is excellent without the bread. Form into a loaf and chill, preferably overnight. Garnish with whole cooked prawns, lemon wedges; scatter Greek olives around the platter and top the loaf alternately with lemon slices and split halves of prawns.

**ARABIC
PICKLED CUCUMBERS**

Wash and pack into hot sterilized 1-pint wide-mouth jar:
4 slender pickling cucumbers, approximately 4 inches long
Sprinkle into jar:
**6 peppercorns
1 teaspoon coriander seeds
3 garlic cloves, slivered
3 to 4 sprigs celery leaves
1 bay leaf, crumbled
1/2 onion, slivered**
Bring to boil:
**1/2 cup each white vinegar and water
1 tablespoon coarse salt**
Pour over cucumbers to cover, seal jar and store in warm place 10 days.
Makes 1 pint

SHIEK NADIM MALLAH, KORANIC SCHOLAR

NORTH OF THE SAHARA

ARABIC
PICKLED TURNIPS

Boil in water until tender; peel, cool, quarter and set aside:
1 large beet
Drop into boiling water for 2 to 3 minutes:
4 small turnips or 3 medium-size turnips, quartered
Remove turnips and peel them. They will have a silky texture. Place in hot sterilized 1-pint wide-mouth jar, packing between each turnip:
1 cooked beet quarter
2 to 3 slivers of garlic clove
2 to 3 sprigs young celery leaves
Combine and bring to boil:
1/2 cup each white vinegar and water
1 tablespoon coarse salt
Fill jar with vinegar mixture, seal and store in warm place 10 days.
Makes 1 pint

MOROCCAN
BRAINS

Wash, cover with water and soak for 15 minutes:
1 pound lamb or calf brains
Remove membranes and veins and run brains under cold running water. Place in boiling water with:
1 onion, quartered
Simmer for 30 minutes. Remove brains from water and drain thoroughly. Cool, slice 1/2 inch thick and arrange on platter. Pour over brains:
3 tablespoons Moroccan salad dressing including tomatoes (following)
Turn slices to coat thoroughly and chill for 1 hour. Remove to serving platter and cover with remaining dressing. Garnish with:
black olives
lemon wedges
Serve as an hors d'oeuvre or salad accompaniment.
Serves 4 to 6

MOROCCAN
SALAD

To the Moroccan, the mixing of spices is a very serious business. Moroccan salads generally consist of one or two ingredients, crowned by a dressing of such subtle and perplexing taste that it is like a guessing game to name the ingredients. Here is one classic Moroccan salad to which I have added my own variations.

Pierce with a fork and grill over an open flame until the skin cracks and blackens:
4 sweet green peppers
2 sweet red peppers
6 large tomatoes
Allow peppers to cool, peel, seed and cut into lengthwise strips. Set aside. Peel tomatoes, cut in half, spoon out seeds, coarsely chop and set aside. Bake in a 350° oven until soft:

4 Japanese eggplants
Cool, slice lengthwise and
season with:
2 teaspoons minced coriander
1/2 teaspoon paprika
1 small dried red chili, crumbled
   (or to taste)
Set aside.
To make dressing, combine in
a bowl:
1/2 cup olive oil
juice of 2 lemons
2 garlic cloves, minced
3 tablespoons minced parsley
1/2 teaspoon cumin
pinch of sugar
salt and freshly ground pepper
   to taste
Add chopped tomatoes to dressing, mix thoroughly and chill for
1 hour. Arrange pepper strips in
a spoke pattern on a serving platter. Place eggplant in the center.
Pour chilled dressing over, distributing evenly. Surround with:
1 large sweet red onion,
   cut in rings
black olives
Serve with:
crisp lettuce leaves
to scoop up salad for eating.
Serves 8 to 10

LENTIL SALAD

Throughout the Middle East you
find lentils in soups, lentils in
stuffing and here are lentils in
the form of a formidable salad.

In water to cover soak overnight:
2 cups brown lentils
Drain and place in kettle with:
water to cover
1 large onion
2 whole cloves
2 bay leaves
2 garlic cloves
1 teaspoon grated fresh
   orange rind
Bring to boil, lower heat and
simmer until tender. Do not
overcook. Add:
salt to taste
Drain, discard onion, cloves, bay
leaves and garlic. Cool. Place in
salad bowl and toss well with
mixture of:
1 cup grated onion
1 cup olive or walnut oil
juice of 2 lemons, or
3 to 4 tablespoons wine vinegar
1/2 teaspoon cumin
freshly ground black pepper
   to taste

Allow to stand 30 minutes
and serve over:
lettuce leaves
Sprinkle with:
minced parsley
Garnish with:
black and green olives
Serves 6 to 8

EGYPTIAN MICHOTETA
(Cucumbers with Feta
Cheese Sauce)

Arrange on bed of lettuce:
2 cucumbers, thinly sliced
2 large mild onions, thinly
   sliced into rings
Combine in blender:
1/4 pound Feta cheese
3 tablespoons olive oil
1 teaspoon minced fresh oregano
1 tablespoon freshly squeezed
   lemon juice or to taste
salt and pepper to taste
Just before serving, pour over
cucumbers and onion.
Serves 4 to 6

111

MOROCCAN EGGPLANT SALAD

Bake in 400° oven until tender:
1 large eggplant
Peel and drain pulp. Mash
pulp with:
2 garlic cloves, mashed
Pound well until thoroughly
mixed. Add:
2 tablespoons minced fresh
 coriander
1/2 teaspoon each salt and
 paprika
pinch cumin
Place pulp mixture in skillet
with:
2 to 3 tablespoons olive oil
Sauté over medium heat, turning
with spatula, until the pulp is the
consistency of mush and liquid
is absorbed.
Turn onto serving platter and
flatten with spatula. Sprinkle
with:
3 tablespoons lemon juice or
 to taste
1 tablespoon olive oil
minced parsley
Garnish with:
tomato wedges
Serve warm or cool.
Serves 4

ARABIC FRESH FRUIT SALAD

Arrange attractively on large
round platter:
fresh orange sections
fresh tangerine sections
apple slices
grapes
peach slices
any fresh fruit in season
Combine:
fruit juice
yoghurt
orange flower water
Pour over and sprinkle with:
chopped walnuts

MOROCCAN HARIRA

Harira is mutton and vegetable soup eaten each day at sundown during Ramadan. It is also sold by street vendors. The flour-and-water thickening agent is sometimes made the day before so that it ferments slightly and adds a musky taste to the soup.

Soak overnight in water to cover:
1/2 cup garbanzo beans
Drain and set aside. Brown lightly in:
4 tablespoons butter
1 pound lean lamb cut into 3/4-inch cubes
wings, backs and giblets from 2 small chickens
1 onion, chopped
1 large celery rib with leaves, chopped
1 to 2 garlic cloves, minced (optional)
1 teaspoon salt
1/2 teaspoon each turmeric and black pepper
1/4 teaspoon cinnamon
1/4 teaspoon powdered ginger or pinch of saffron

Add reserved garbanzo beans and:
2 quarts water or chicken or lamb stock
1/2 cup or more chopped parsley
4 large ripe tomatoes, peeled and chopped
1/2 cup lentils, well washed
Bring to boil, lower heat, cover and simmer 30 minutes.
Add:
1/4 cup long-grain rice
1/4 cup chopped fresh coriander (optional)
12 small white onions
Cover and continue cooking 20 minutes, adding last 8 minutes:
1/2 cup thin noodles or vermicelli
Make a thin paste of:
1/4 cup water
3 tablespoons lemon juice
3 tablespoons flour

Last 3 minutes of cooking gradually add paste to soup. Cook and stir until slightly thickened. Remove chicken, skin, bone and chop. Return to soup and adjust seasonings to taste. Transfer to heated soup tureen and float on top:
lemon slices sprinkled with paprika
Serve with side dish of eggs lightly seasoned with saffron, cumin and salt and softly scrambled.
Serves 6 to 8
Variation
Omit flour binder. Beat together:
2 eggs, beaten
3 tablespoons lemon juice
Gradually stir into hot soup to make strands. Remove from heat, adjust seasonings and serve with pita bread.

NORTH OF THE SAHARA

EGYPTIAN MILOOKHIYYA SOUP

Combine and bring to boil:
1 chicken, approximately
    4 pounds
2 onions, quartered
3 garlic cloves, mashed
2 celery ribs and leaves, chopped
6 parsley sprigs
4 ripe tomatoes, chopped
1 tablespoon salt
8 peppercorns, lightly crushed
6 whole allspice, lightly
    crushed
2 quarts water
Cover, lower heat and simmer
until chicken is tender. Remove
chicken, remove chicken meat
from bones and reserve. Return
bones to soup. Continue cooking
30 minutes. Strain broth and
return to pot. Adjust seasonings.
Place in bowl:
1 to 2 cups dried milookhiyya*,
    crumbled
warm water to cover
1 teaspoon lemon juice

Let soak 20 minutes or until
almost double in bulk. Drain and
add to broth. Bring to boil and
cook over medium heat, stirring
so leaves do not fall to bottom,
20 to 30 minutes. While cooking,
prepare garlic paste. Melt over
low heat until foamy:
3 tablespoons butter
Crush together:
4 to 5 garlic cloves
1 teaspoon powdered coriander
1/4 teaspoon allspice
1/8 teaspoon cayenne pepper or
    to taste
Add garlic paste to butter and
cook until just golden. Just
before serving soup, add garlic
butter and cook 2 minutes.
Serve soup with:
reserved chicken meat heated
    in a little broth
steamed rice (see Basics)
Serves 6 to 8
*Milookhiyya is a leafy vegetable
available dried in Middle Eastern
stores. It is sometimes called
Spanish okra. Fresh sorrel or
spinach may be substituted, but
should not be soaked.

MOROCCAN RICE

To basic steamed rice (see Basics)
add:
3 tablespoons sultanas (soaked
    in water)
1/4 cup toasted chopped
    hazelnuts
Toss well with fork, place on
heated serving platter and top
with:
1 cup onion rings, browned until
    crisp in
3 tablespoons butter

CAIRO PILAV

Prepare as directed:
double recipe basic steamed
    rice made with curry (see
    Basics)
Toss in and mix well with fork:
1/2 cup each sultanas or currants,
    plumped in water, and toasted
    slivered blanched almonds
Adjust seasonings with:
salt and pepper
Fluff with fork and turn out
onto heated platter.
Serves 4 to 6

KUWAITI BOOM DHOW

NORTH OF THE SAHARA

NORTH AFRICAN RICE, SPINACH AND LENTIL PILAF

This is my own combination pilaf of lentils, rice and spinach, all of which are eaten profusely in North Africa, and there are a number of variations. The tastes of all are excellent for the Western palate. A healthful combination to complement any dish or a meal in itself.

In a large skillet sauté until golden in:
4 tablespoons butter or olive oil
1 cup minced onions
Add, stir and cook gently until heated:
4 cups cooked lentils (see Basics)
4 cups steamed rice (see Basics)
In a separate skillet sauté until golden in:
4 tablespoons butter or olive oil
1/2 cup minced onion
Add to skillet and cook just until wilted:
3 bunches spinach, trimmed and shredded

Toss spinach into lentil-rice mixture and blend ingredients briefly over low heat. Mound on large heated serving platter. Sauté until transparent and slightly crisp in:
4 tablespoons butter or olive oil
2 onions, thinly sliced in rings
Pour onions over pilaf and serve with bread.
Serves 8 as a main meal

ARABIC FRUIT-STUFFED TOMATOES

Cut 1/2-inch tops off:
4 large tomatoes
Reserve tops and scoop out pulp of tomatoes, leaving a 1/2-inch shell. Place upside down to drain. Chop half the pulp and set aside. Reserve rest of pulp for another use.
Sauté until onions are transparent in:
2 tablespoons vegetable oil
3/4 cup minced onion
Blend in:
2 cups steamed rice (see Basics)
1 cup mixed sultanas, chopped walnuts, blanched almonds and pistachio nuts in any combination or proportions
1/2 cup chopped dried fruits (any combination) that have been softened in hot water

reserved tomato pulp
2 tablespoons orange marmalade
2 tablespoons lemon juice
1 tablespoon each chopped fresh mint and honey
1/2 teaspoon each allspice and cinnamon
1/4 teaspoon salt
Adjust seasonings to taste.
Sprinkle inside of tomatoes with:
salt
Rub inside and out with:
honey
Stuff tomatoes with rice mixture. Place any leftover stuffing in bottom of baking pan, place tomatoes on top and drizzle over mixture of:
1/4 cup orange marmalade
2 tablespoons honey
Sprinkle lightly with:
cinnamon
Bake in 350° oven, basting often, 20 minutes or until tender. Chill. Serve cold as a first course or accompaniment for fowl.
Serves 4

"FIGHT THOSE WHO BELIEVE NOT IN GOD, NOR THE LAST DAY"

MOROCCAN COUSCOUS-STUFFED TURNIPS

Cut 1/2-inch tops off:
4 to 6 very large sweet turnips
Cut a sliver off bottom so they will stand in pan; scoop out pulp, leaving a 1/4-inch shell. Chop half the pulp and set aside. Reserve remainder for another use. Cover shells with:
boiling salted water
Cover and simmer gently 10 minutes. Drain, peel and set aside.

Sauté until onions are transparent in:
4 tablespoons butter
1 large onion, grated
reserved chopped turnip pulp
1 tablespoon chopped parsley
1/2 teaspoon each powdered ginger and turmeric
Add and continue cooking 10 minutes to blend flavors:
1 cup sultanas and chopped, dried apricots, figs and dates in any combination, softened in boiling water and drained

Remove from heat and add:
1 cup couscous steamed as directed on page 121 with fruit juices instead of water
1/4 cup mixed chopped blanched almonds and walnuts
Stuff turnips and place in buttered baking dish. Sprinkle with:
pomegranate seeds (if available)
Cover and bake in 350° oven 35 minutes or until tender. May be served hot or cold as a vegetable or as a garnish or first course.
Serves 4 to 6

117

PASTILLA
(Also Bisteeya, Bastilla)

Pastilla, pastilla, thy name is sweet. To those of you who seek new horizons of taste, pastilla will end your quest. Made with tissue-thin pastry dough (similar to Chinese spring roll dough) called warka, this rich and elegant dish from Fez takes time and effort, but the results are worth it. I have substituted phyllo dough for the warka which works almost as well. In Morocco, the pastilla is traditionally filled with pigeon meat, small birds which abound there. Some substitute chicken for the pigeon, though I prefer the tender, succulent meat of Cornish hens.

Wash well and pat dry inside and out, reserving giblets:

3 Cornish hens

Rub well inside and out with paste of:

4 garlic cloves, minced

1 tablespoon salt

Let stand 10 minutes and then place hens and giblets into a saucepan in which they fit snugly. Combine:

1 teaspoon finely minced ginger root

1 teaspoon coriander

1/2 teaspoon coarsely ground black pepper

1/4 teaspoon turmeric

pinch saffron

1 cup hot water

Pour over hens and add water to cover. Sprinkle on top:

3 cinnamon sticks

1 large onion, finely minced

1 cup minced parsley

1/4 pound butter, cut into bits

Bring to boil, cover, lower heat and cook 1 hour or until hens are tender. Let cool in stock, remove and shred meat and giblets into small pieces. Set aside. In heavy skillet brown in:

3 tablespoons butter

1-1/2 cups blanched almonds

Drain on paper toweling, cool and chop finely. Combine with:

1/4 cup powdered sugar

2 teaspoons cinnamon

Set almond mixture aside. Remove the cinnamon sticks from the stock and cook stock over medium-high heat until reduced to 1-1/2 cups. Lower heat to medium and add:

3 tablespoons lemon juice

Keep at simmer and gradually beat in:

6 eggs, beaten until frothy

Cook, stirring constantly, 10 minutes, or until eggs are cooked but not dry. Remove from heat and season with:

salt to taste

Stack on a cookie sheet:

4 phyllo sheets

Bake in a 400° oven 1 minute, so leaves are crisp but not browned. Set aside. Using 9 phyllo sheets and approximately 3/4 cup butter, follow directions on page 138 for working with phyllo dough. Spread an iron 12-inch skillet lavishly with melted butter and arrange 6 buttered phyllo sheets in the pan, letting edges hang over the sides. Fold another buttered sheet and place in center of skillet. Sprinkle with:

reserved almond mixture

Cover with:

half the egg mixture

Top with:

2 of the baked phyllo sheets

Layer over sheets:

reserved Cornish hen meat and giblets

Top with:

remaining baked phyllo sheets

Cover with:

remaining egg mixture

Fold edges of dough over and brush with melted butter. Arrange remaining 2 unbaked phyllo sheets on top, tucking edges in under pie to enclose completely. Brush with melted butter. Bake in a 425° oven 20 minutes, or until golden brown. Shake pan slightly, loosen edges of pie with spatula and invert on buttered cookie sheet, pouring off any excess butter and reserving it. Brush top with reserved butter and bake approximately 10 minutes, or until golden. Remove from oven and sprinkle lavishly with:

sifted powdered sugar

Make a crisscross pattern on top with:

ground cinnamon

Slide onto heated serving plate and serve immediately.

Serves 10 to 12

NORTH OF THE SAHARA

ARABIC STUFFED ONIONS

Peel and remove first layer of:
6 large onions
Being careful not to overcook, boil onions in salted water until barely tender. Cool and lift out centers, leaving a 1/2-inch shell. Turn upside down to drain. Chop 3/4ths of the center and combine with:
2 cups hot steamed rice (see Basics; use water)
1/2 cup each chopped walnuts and currants
2 large tart green apples, grated
3 tablespoons each ginger preserves and orange flower water
1 teaspoon salt
1/4 teaspoon each allspice and pepper
Adjust seasonings. Stuff onion shells and place in baking pan. Pour into pan:
1 cup water
3/4 cup fruit juice
Bake in 300° oven 25 minutes, basting several times during cooking.
Serves 6

TUNISIAN BRIK (Fried Egg Pies)

In North Africa, brik are made with warka, a dough similar to the paper-thin Chinese spring roll skins. I have substituted phyllo dough. The filling can be almost anything, such as ground meat and tomatoes, with an egg always included. Form the square to fit the filling.

Work with 1 sheet of phyllo at a time (see Basics). Brush with melted butter and fold into a 5-inch square.
Break into center:
1 small or medium-sized egg
Sprinkle with:
1 teaspoon minced parsley
1 teaspoon minced chives
salt and freshly ground pepper
Quickly fold over to make triangle, sealing edges with more melted butter if needed. Heat peanut oil to about 400° and deep fry, one at a time, on both sides until golden, turning once. Drain on paper toweling and serve immediately.

MOROCCAN BRAINS AND EGGS

Wash, cover with water and soak 15 minutes:
1 pound lamb or calf brains
Remove membranes and veins and run brains under cold running water. Place in boiling water with:
1 onion, quartered
Simmer for 30 minutes. Remove brains from water and drain thoroughly. Cool, slice 1/2 inch thick and layer half of the slices in a well-buttered casserole.
Spoon over top:
half of Moroccan salad dressing including tomatoes (page 110)
Cover with remaining brain slices and remaining dressing. Beat until frothy:
8 eggs
Pour eggs over brains and bake at 350° for 35 minutes, or until eggs are set. Remove from oven and allow to cool slightly. Cut in squares and serve.
Serves 4 to 6

COUSCOUS

Couscous, the national dish of North Africa, is a type of fine semolina made from wheat grain. Though a domestically-produced semolina is available in this country, it is not of a type that can be used for making this dish. North African couscous is imported packaged to this country, and is available at Middle Eastern stores, Greek delicatessens and in gourmet sections of supermarkets. The instructions for cooking couscous are on the package, but I pray, do not follow them. It will rob you of an opportunity to experience the pleasure of eating couscous prepared as the North Africans do. There is no similarity between the results.

If it is within your means purchase a couscoussière, the pot traditionally used in the making of couscous. It is generally made of aluminum or stainless steel and has two parts. The bottom pan is large, round-sided and deep and is where the tagine, or stew, is cooked, or in some cases where water or fruit juice is simmered. The smaller top pan where the couscous is cooked is like a strainer with rather large holes, and fits snugly into the lower pan. A couscoussière can be improvised with pots you already have. Use a deep round pan for the lower compartment and a cheesecloth-lined colander that fits tightly into it for the upper pan. Because of the amount of ingredients and time involved in making couscous and tagine, their preparation is well suited for entertaining large gatherings. Invite your friends to participate in the preparation. It is a conversation piece and the result is an exciting culinary experience.

The first time I made couscous I used the directions on the package with disastrous results. Then I met Maureen Daniels, born in Tunisia and raised in Morocco. She taught me the secret to making a delicious couscous, which I impart to you now.

BASIC METHOD OF STEAMING COUSCOUS

Let couscous soak in cold water 5 minutes, fluffing once with fingertips. Place in couscoussière or cheesecloth-lined colander or steamer. Steam over water, fruit juices or over stews for 15 minutes. Remove couscous to large platter and roll grains between open palms with melted butter for sweet couscous, olive or vegetable oil for stew couscous. Continue rubbing until grains are completely coated and separate. Return to couscoussière and steam 10 minutes longer or until tender and fluffy. When steaming, always wrap lid of couscoussière or steamer in a tea towel to prevent condensation. Remove to plate and with fork toss with melted butter. Proceed with recipe.

CONSERIE D'HARISSA

With a mortar and pestle, grind together:
2 tablespoons cayenne pepper
1 tablespoon cumin
2 garlic cloves, minced
1/2 teaspoon salt
Store in the refrigerator in a glass jar with a tight-fitting lid.
Variation
To make harissa sauce, add 1 cup olive oil to the above mixture and cook, stirring constantly, 5 minutes. Serve with couscous dishes.

NORTH OF THE SAHARA

TAGINE

The tagine is the stew of Morocco. The Israelis have their chollet, the Syrians and Lebanese their yakhnie, the Persians their abgusht. But it is the Moroccan tagine that has given to the humble stew some of its greatest glory. The combining of fruit or vegetables with meats in the Moroccan manner will result in a delicious blending of flavors and aromas foreign yet pleasant to the Western palate.

The ingredients of a tagine vary regionally and seasonally. When fresh fruits are in season, utilize them. Added midway to the completion of a tagine, the fruit will be absorbed and their fresh tang will linger. When dried fruits are used they are put into the pot at the beginning of the cooking of the tagine, resulting in a creamy syrup-like sauce.

I have chosen to include here tagines of outstanding taste, each made with a distinctive array of ingredients. These tagines are a result of recipes given to me by various Arabic-speaking people, and my own extensive testing. Once you have cooked a tagine served with couscous, the results will be blessed by Allah.

122

COUSCOUS TAGINE

Sauté to gently brown in:
1/4 cup olive oil
1 pound lamb, cut in large pieces
1 2- to 3-pound chicken, cut into pieces
2 onions, cut into chunks
4 carrots, thickly sliced
Place in large stewing pot or bottom of couscoussière. Add:
chicken stock to cover
3 celery ribs, cut into large chunks
3 cinnamon sticks
10 peppercorns, lightly crushed
10 whole cloves
1 teaspoon cumin
1 to 2 teaspoons conserie d'harissa (page 121)
1/8 teaspoon powdered saffron
1-1/2 teaspoons salt
1/2 teaspoon freshly ground black pepper
4 ripe tomatoes, peeled and cut up
Cover and cook 10 minutes. Add:
2 cups cooked garbanzo beans (see Basics)
2 sweet potatoes, peeled and cut into chunks
2 turnips, peeled and cut into chunks

Cover and continue cooking 20 minutes. Follow directions for steaming couscous (preceding), using:
2 cups couscous
3 tablespoons olive oil after first steaming
Before returning couscous to complete steaming process, add to stew:
1 pound zucchini, cut into large chunks
1 pound artichoke hearts, chokes removed and cut into quarters (optional)
Let couscous steam 10 minutes or until tender. Remove to plate and with fork toss in:
4 tablespoons melted butter
1 teaspoon salt
Arrange couscous on heated platter and make a hollow in center. Pour stew into center, removing cinnamon sticks.
Sprinkle all with:
1 cup pine nuts
Garnish with:
moistened dried apricots
fresh grapes
lemon wedges
Serves 8 to 10

BREAKING CAMP AT DAWN

NORTH OF THE SAHARA

CHICKEN TAGINE WITH QUINCE AND ALMONDS

Quince and almonds, the classic affinity, combined with chicken and the spices of Morocco produce the quintessence of taste. Quince is not always available. Therefore this version uses the imported quince preserves available in Middle Eastern stores.

Halve:
2 2-pound chickens
Rub well with:
salt
pepper
cinnamon
Brown on both sides in:
1/4 pound butter
Place in heavy Dutch oven and pour butter from skillet over halves. Sprinkle with:
3 slices candied ginger, grated
Add:
1 teaspoon almond extract, mixed with
2 cups chicken broth
Cover and cook, turning several times, over low heat until chicken is tender. In sautéing skillet brown in:
2 tablespoons butter
1 large onion, grated
1/4 cup chopped fresh coriander or parsley

124

Add:
1 large cooking apple, grated
3 slices candied ginger, grated
2 tablespoons lemon juice
1/4 teaspoon saffron or to taste dissolved in
2 tablespoons orange flower water
1 2-inch stick cinnamon
1 teaspoon salt
1/2 teaspoon freshly ground black pepper
Cook and stir 10 minutes, adding if needed for sauce consistency:
chicken broth
Blend in:
1 cup quince preserves
Adjust seasonings with more saffron or ginger, salt and pepper. Sauce must not be too highly seasoned so that the quince flavor can predominate. Lower fire and simmer 20 minutes, stirring occasionally and adding broth as needed. Remove chicken halves to heated platter, disjointing if desired. Pour juices from chicken into quince sauce and blend well.
Add to sauce:
1 cup blanched almonds browned in
3 tablespoons butter
Pour sauce over chicken and garnish with:
apple wedges
Serve with couscous.
Serves 4

BEEF TAGINE WITH LENTILS

This beef tagine is reminiscent of the Jewish chollet. Served on a bed of lentils, an unusual, pleasant taste is created.

Rub well with:
salt and pepper
1/2 teaspoon each cinnamon and paprika
1 4- to 5-pound brisket of beef
Brown on all sides in:
4 tablespoons butter
Add and simmer over low fire until onions are tender:
2 onions, minced
Add:
2 large apples, grated
2 cups unpitted prunes
1 pound pearl onions
2 tablespoons sugar
3/4 cup whole or slivered blanched almonds
3 slivers lemon peel
water to cover
Cover, bring to gentle boil and simmer, basting often, 2 hours or until meat is tender.
Serve with sauce on bed of:
cooked lentils (see Basics)
Garnish with:
blanched almonds
apple wedges
Serves 8

EGYPTIAN
PLAKI FISH

Soak 30 minutes or more and set aside:

1 cup sultanas or raisins
water or white wine to cover

Prepare for cooking and rub with:

salt and pepper
1 3- to 4-pound whole fish, preferably bass, or
4 1-inch thick halibut steaks

Sprinkle with:

juice of 2 lemons

Set aside. Sauté until tender in:

1/2 cup olive oil
3 onions, sliced
1 cup chopped whites of leeks (optional)
1/2 cup each chopped parsley and celery
3 garlic cloves, minced

Add and mix well:

6 ripe tomatoes, peeled and chopped, or
1 16-ounce can tomatoes, chopped

Reheat and season to taste with:

salt and pepper

Place half tomato mixture in shallow baking dish. Place fish on bed of mixture and pour remaining sauce over. Sprinkle with:

2 tablespoons chopped fresh oregano

Tuck into sauce:

3 bay leaves

Pour over fish:

reserved raisins and their liquid
1 cup additional water or white wine for whole fish, or
2/3 cup for steaks

Bake, basting frequently, in 350° oven 45 minutes or until fish flakes easily with fork. If using steaks, bake only 20 to 30 minutes. Last 5 minutes of cooking, add to sauce to absorb juices:

12 whole prawns, cooked, shelled and deveined

When fish is done, remove prawns and reserve for garnish. Place fish on heated serving platter, pour juices over and garnish with reserved prawns and:

lemon slices

Serve with:

rice pilaff (see Basics)

Serves 4

MOROCCAN
STUFFED BASS

Sprinkle inside and out with salt and pepper and set aside:

1 3-pound bass

Sauté until transparent in:

1 tablespoon butter
2 large onions, grated

Spread on bottom of buttered baking dish and set aside.

Make a paste by combining:

1/2 cup finely ground almonds
1 teaspoon sugar
1/2 teaspoon cinnamon
1/4 teaspoon cumin
2 tablespoons each soft sweet butter and almond paste
3 tablespoons imported quince preserves

Spread paste onto fish with spatula, covering thoroughly and smoothly. Place fish on onion bed and pour around fish in pan:

1/2 cup water

Bake in 350° oven 45 minutes or until done. A crust should form on the fish. Remove to serving platter; surround with pan juices and garnish with:

lemon wedges
parsley sprigs

Serves 6

WOVEN PALM
SUN CAP PRO-
TECTS ARAB
FARMER

TUNISIAN SEA BASS CASSEROLE

Wash and pat dry:
2 pounds sea bass fillets or steaks
Place fish in baking pan and
sprinkle with:
salt and pepper
juice of 2 lemons
1/4 cup olive oil
Turn fillets to evenly coat with
juices. Sauté until transparent in:
4 tablespoons olive oil
2 large onions, thinly sliced
Add:
6 large ripe tomatoes, dropped
    in boiling water, peeled and
    chopped
12 small new potatoes, parboiled
    and peeled
12 pearl onions, dropped in
    boiling water and peeled
2 cups cooked garbanzos (see
    Basics)
2 cups fish stock or clam juice
1/4 teaspoon each powdered
    saffron and cayenne pepper
Simmer until potatoes and
onions are tender. Adjust with
salt and pepper. Pour mixture
over fish and sprinkle over it:
2 tablespoons olive oil
1 cup sultanas

Bake in 350° oven 30 minutes, adding more fish or clam broth if needed and basting several times. Remove from oven and arrange fillets on serving platter. Spoon sauce and vegetables over and garnish with:

cooked shrimp
lemon wedges

Or fillets and vegetables may be served in individual casseroles. Serves 4

WHOLE FISH WITH DRIED FRUIT STUFFING

This splendid dish is suitable for special occasions for dinner or buffet. Although salmon is not available in the Middle East, it lends itself to this recipe and may be substituted for the shad.

Wash, scale and dry:

1 5-pound shad with head and tail intact

Halve lengthwise, remove bone and sew spine back together with needle and thread. Sprinkle inside and out with:

salt and pepper

Set aside. Combine into a paste:

1/4 cup olive oil
1 teaspoon grated ginger root
2 tablespoons almond paste
1 teaspoon allspice

Rub mixture well into inside and outside of shad and refrigerate. In saucepan combine:

8 pitted figs
8 pitted dates
8 pitted prunes
8 apricots
1 tablespoon lemon juice
water to cover

Bring to boil, remove from heat and remove fruits with slotted spoon. Set aside and reserve juices.

Bring to boil:

1/2 cup water
pinch salt

Add:

1-1/2 teaspoons sweet butter
3-1/2 tablespoons rice flour

Cover and simmer 20 minutes. Remove from heat and let cool; it should have a creamy consistency. Blend in well into mixture:

3/4 cup finely ground almonds, pistachio nuts, walnuts in any combination and proportion
1 tablespoon butter, softened
1/2 teaspoon each sugar, cinnamon and allspice

Make an indentation in each of the reserved fruits and stuff with nut mixture, carefully securing each fruit closed after stuffing. Place 5 of each of the stuffed fruits in rows in cavity of fish. Sew or skewer fish securely. Make a bed in baking dish with mixture of:

3 large onions, grated
2 tablespoons olive oil
2 teaspoons grated ginger root
1/2 teaspoon salt
1/4 teaspoon black pepper

Place stuffed fish on bed and surround with remaining fruit. Brush fish with:

4 tablespoons melted butter

Pour around fish:

1 cup reserved juice in which fruits were cooked

Cover with foil and bake in 350° oven 1 hour. Remove foil, raise heat to 400° and cook for additional 15 minutes or until well browned and tender. Carefully transfer fish to large serving platter and pour pan juices around it. Place stuffed fruit around fish and garnish edge of platter with alternating lemon and orange slices. Serves 8 to 10

NORTH OF THE SAHARA

EGYPTIAN STUFFED VEAL ROLL

Boil until tongues are tender:
6 lamb tongues
water to cover
1 onion, sliced
1 bay leaf
1/2 teaspoon salt
1/4 teaspoon pepper
Remove tongues, slice and place in large pan. Strain and reserve cooking water.
Lay on board and pound to flatten:
1 boned leg of veal, approximately 4 pounds
Cut off high spots and fill low spots to make as even as possible. Place veal in pan with sliced tongue and pour over it a mixture of:
1 cup reserved cooking water
1/2 cup olive oil
juice of 2 lemons
1 large onion, thinly sliced
2 garlic cloves, mashed
3 bay leaves, crumbled
3 tablespoons minced parsley
1/2 teaspoon each turmeric, powdered coriander and salt
1 teaspoon almond paste
1/4 teaspoon black pepper

Marinate, turning often, overnight. Remove veal and lay flat on board. Remove tongue and onions from marinade and finely mince or purée in blender with 2 or more tablespoons reserved marinade. Combine with:
2 cups chopped cooked artichoke hearts, mashed (optional)
Adjust seasonings to taste and spread mixture over veal and sprinkle with:
1/2 cup chopped pistachio nuts
Starting on one long edge, roll like jelly roll, tucking in ends and tying firmly with twine. Place in saucepan to fit snugly. Pour marinade over, adding to cover:
reserved cooking water and/or chicken stock
Bring to gentle boil, cover, lower heat and simmer, basting often, about 2 hours. Remove veal and place on plate. Weigh down with heavy lid and refrigerate overnight. Remove twine, slice 1/4 inch thick and arrange on serving platter. Serve chilled.
Serves 12

FISH TARATOR

Wrap in heavy foil:
1 3- to 4-pound whole bass, cleaned but with skin left on
1 onion, chopped
1 garlic clove, minced
1 bay leaf
3 tablespoons each lemon juice, olive oil and water
1/2 teaspoon salt
1/4 teaspoon black pepper
Bake in 350° oven 35 minutes or until fish flakes easily. Cool, cut off head and tail and set them aside. Flake fish finely and combine with:
1/2 cup raisins soaked in water to cover
1/4 cup pine nuts browned in butter
1/4 cup finely minced onion
1-1/2 tablespoons lemon juice
3 tablespoons minced parsley
salt and pepper to taste
Mound on serving platter and shape into fish form. Cover with:
tarator sauce (following)
Place head and tail in position and form an eye with a black olive half. Garnish fish with:
pitted dates
dried apricot halves
Serves 6 to 8

TARATOR SAUCE

Soak in:
water, fish stock or clam juice
2 cups croutons
Place in blender with:
1/2 cup each chopped blanched
   almonds and pine nuts
1 to 2 garlic cloves, minced
3 tablespoons lemon juice
2 tablespoons olive oil
salt and pepper to taste
Makes approximately 1-1/2 cups

BEDOUIN HOSPITALITY

Imagine roaming the North African desert, where grass is often scarce and water scarcer still. Here, a Sheik's son pours a cup of coffee unparalleled for potency in the Western world. It is interesting and timely to note that shortly after the introduction of coffee to the Europeans, laws were established proscribing its possession or use. Penalties were quite severe, often entailing mutilation and infrequently, death.

BEDOUIN HOSPITALITY

NORTH OF THE SAHARA

TETUANESE VERSIA
(Cornish Hens with Tomato Jam)

This Middle Eastern recipe intrigued me and I tried it using Cornish hens rather than the traditional chicken with excellent results. All small birds are delicate and need not be burdened by heavy sauces. This combination of sweetened tomatoes and a touch of saffron is a tantalizing taste. Excellent for two or more and easily prepared.

Dry inside and out:
2 Cornish hens
Rub inside and out with:
1/2 garlic clove, mashed
salt and pepper
Sprinkle with:
1 teaspoon grated ginger root
Set aside. Combine:
1 10-ounce jar imported tomato
    preserves
2 large ripe tomatoes, peeled
    and chopped
1 tablespoon each orange honey,
    orange flower water and
    grated crystallized ginger
1/2 teaspoon cinnamon
pinch of powdered saffron

Butter a baking pan and make a bed with 2 to 3 tablespoons of tomato mixture. Place hens in pan and pour remaining tomato mixture over. Cover loosely with foil and bake in 300° oven 30 minutes. Remove foil, raise heat to 375°, baste and cook an additional 15 minutes, or until tender and browned.
Transfer birds to serving platter, cover with sauce and keep warm. In a skillet melt:
1 tablespoon butter
Add and brown:
1 tablespoon each slivered
    blanched almonds and
    sesame seeds
Pour over birds and garnish with:
lemon wedges
Serve with steamed rice.
Serves 4

CHICKEN WITH OLIVES

Bring to boil:
1 cup each unpitted Kalamata
    black olives and green Greek
    olives
water to cover
Strain and set aside. Split in half and pat dry:
2 small fryers, approximately
    2 pounds each

Place chicken halves in baking pan that has been brushed with olive oil and squeeze over them:
juice of 2 lemons
Grate over top of chicken:
4 pieces crystallized ginger
Combine:
1/4 cup olive oil
2 garlic cloves, mashed
1/4 cup orange blossom honey
1 tablespoon orange flower water
pinch of saffron
Brush chickens lavishly with mixture and broil 15 to 20 minutes, basting several times with pastry brush during broiling, or until delicately browned. Remove from broiler and surround chicken with reserved olives, brushing them with basting mixture to coat well. Bake in 350° oven 20 minutes, or until tender, basting and turning the olives several times and basting the chicken.
Transfer chicken to heated serving platter and surround with olives that have been lifted out with slotted spoon. Pour pan juices over all and garnish with:
lemon wedges
Serve with steamed rice made with saffron (see Basics).
Serves 4
Note: It is important that unpitted olives be used because of their superior flavor.

EGYPTIAN
OKRA LAMB CASSEROLE

Lamb and okra are a classic Egyptian favorite. I prefer the frozen okra which are always available and are not as time consuming in preparation.

Sauté until soft in:
6 tablespoons butter
2 large onions, minced
1 garlic clove, minced
1 tablespoon minced parsley
Add and brown:
2 pounds ground lean lamb
   (or beef)
1/2 teaspoon salt
1/4 teaspoon pepper
1 teaspoon minced fresh
   oregano, or
1 tablespoon minced fresh mint
1/2 teaspoon ground coriander
   (optional)
Blend in:
3 tablespoons tomato paste
Adjust seasonings. Simmer over low heat until juices are absorbed. Set aside.
Gently sauté until starting to soften in:
4 tablespoons butter
1 16-ounce package frozen okra, defrosted and patted dry, or
1 pound fresh okra

Set aside. Add to meat mixture:
1/2 cup bread crumbs
2 eggs, beaten
Pack meat mixture into large, heavy, well-buttered casserole and drizzle over it:
4 tablespoons burnt butter
Arrange okra on top of meat in spoke fashion, forming a pyramid. Pour over casserole:
3 tablespoons lemon juice
Dot with:
2 tablespoons butter
Cover and bake in 350° oven 45 minutes. Remove from oven, cool slightly and serve from casserole accompanied with pilaff and garnish with:
lemon wedges
Serves 8

MOROCCAN
MECHOUI
(Roast Suckling Lamb)

Have your butcher prepare a suckling lamb for roasting. Wash and dry the lamb well. Combine to form a paste:
2 tablespoons ground coriander
5 garlic cloves, mashed
2 teaspoons cumin
1-1/2 teaspoons paprika
salt and freshly ground pepper
   to taste
1/4 pound butter, softened

Rub half of the paste mixture onto the inside and outside of lamb. Place the lamb on a rotating spit, securing spit tightly against backbone and tying legs well. Roast from 6 to 12 inches over bed of glowing charcoal, basting lamb frequently with remaining paste. Watch carefully to be sure forequarters are not cooking too quickly, adjusting coals accordingly. The total cooking time should be about 2-1/2 to 3 hours, depending on the size of the lamb and the heat of the coals. When done, it should be brown and crisp on the outside and tender on the inside. Remove from spit and let rest before cutting. Place on a platter or wooden board and garnish with:
clusters of fresh coriander

NORTH OF THE SAHARA

ALMOND COOKIES

Cream:
1/2 pound sweet butter, softened
Sift:
2-1/2 cups pastry flour
1 cup powdered sugar
Blend into butter and stir in:
1/2 teaspoon each orange flower
water and almond extract*
1 egg yolk, beaten
2 tablespoons milk
Dough will be crumbly. With
fingers form into 1-inch balls.
Roll in palms of hands to smooth
and flatten slightly. Onto each
flattened ball press:
1 whole blanched almond
Bake on cookie sheet in 350° oven
10 minutes or until just starting
to turn golden. Remove from
cookie sheet and cool on rack.
Store in air-tight tin.
Makes approximately 3-1/2 dozen
*Anise water may be substituted
for the almond extract.

PITA BREAD

Dissolve in:
1-1/4 cups warm water
1 yeast cake or 1 tablespoon
dry yeast
Blend in:
3 cups flour, sifted with
1-1/2 teaspoons salt
Turn out on floured board and
knead thoroughly, adding flour
as needed and using enough
melted butter or oil to moisten
hands. Divide dough into 6 balls,
knead each ball well and roll on
floured board into a disc about
5 inches in diameter and 1/4
inch thick. Sprinkle a tea towel
lightly with flour. Place pita
discs on one-half, sprinkle them
very lightly with flour and fold
tea towel over top. Let rise 30 to
45 minutes or until 1-1/2 times
their size. Heat oiled cookie
sheets in 500° oven. When heated,
place discs on sheets and bake in
500° oven 10 to 15 minutes.
Bread will puff up and seem hard,
but will soften when cool. Slice
or separate to make pockets for
various delectable fillings.
Makes 6 discs

MOROCCAN BREAD

Dissolve in:
1/4 cup lukewarm water
1 yeast cake or 1 tablespoon
dry yeast
Add to yeast:
2 teaspoons sugar
Set aside for 5 minutes until
foamy. In large mixing bowl sift
together:
approximately 3 to 4 cups
unbleached white flour
1 cup whole-wheat flour
1 teaspoon salt
Make a well in center of flour
mixture and pour in:
dissolved yeast
3/4 cup lukewarm milk
4 tablespoons melted butter
2 tablespoons orange flower water
1 tablespoon each anise seeds
and sesame seeds
Mix well and turn out onto
floured board. Knead well until
elastic and smooth, distributing
seeds evenly. Form into 2 balls.
Place each ball in a well-buttered
bowl and work with hands into
a cone shape. Sprinkle a large
cookie sheet with cornmeal and
place cones upside down on sheet.

Flatten to form a disc approximately 7 inches in diameter. Cover with slightly dampened tea towel and let rise in warm place 3 hours or until almost double in bulk. Make shallow slashes around edge of loaves in half-moon shape. Bake in preheated 400° oven 10 minutes. Lower heat to 350° and continue baking 30 minutes or until bread sounds hollow when tapped on the bottom. Cool on rack and cut in wedges. Bread will have a heavy consistency.
Makes 2 loaves

ANTAR . . . BEDOUIN POET, LOVER AND CHAMPION

Antar was the son of a sheik and a black African slave, a rather daring move for the 13th century. Antar's skin favored his mother's side of the family, further complicating matters when Antar fell in love with his uncle's daughter, who was as white as the newly driven sand. Thus it was that Antar was relegated to the position of camel herder and sent into the desert, where he somehow managed to locate and organize an army of underdogs, thereby assuring himself a generous degree of public empathy.

ANTAR ... BEDOUIN POET, LOVER, AND CHAMPION

NORTH OF THE SAHARA

ATAIF

Ataif is the crêpe of the Middle East, with as many different kinds of fillings as the more well-known French crêpe. It is traditionally served with eishta, a type of clotted cream which cannot be duplicated with complete success with our commercial cream. It requires an hour of constant boiling and stirring and then 24 hours of refrigeration. A layer then forms on the top which is removed and eaten with crepes or other sweets. I have substituted whipped cream for the eishta. My mother taught me to make the Greek crêpe, tignites, which was first fried and then dipped in syrup. This Egyptian crêpe has a different preparation, but the result is an equally delicious dessert. You may use your own favorite crêpe batter recipe and add a tablespoon of rose water to it.

Combine and mix well:

1-1/2 cups sifted all-purpose flour
2 teaspoons finely granulated sugar
1-1/2 cups lukewarm milk
2 eggs, lightly beaten
2 tablespoons melted butter
1-1/2 tablespoons rose water or orange flower water

Place mixture in blender and blend at high speed for about 2 minutes, or until smooth. Refrigerate for 2 hours. When ready to use, stir well and dilute with a little water if batter is too thick. Heat a heavy cast iron or aluminum skillet, approximately 7 inches in diameter. With a paper towel, brush heated pan with vegetable oil to make a light coating. Spoon about 1 tablespoon of batter into the pan and tilt the pan to completely coat bottom, forming a round thin crêpe. Cook until edges are lightly browned and top is dry. Turn with spatula to cook other side. Repeat until all batter is used, stacking the crepes as they are cooked. Use at once or store in the refrigerator up to 2 days.

To fill 18 crêpes, have ready:

1 10-ounce jar imported rose petal preserves
1/2 cup chopped pistachios
1 pint whipping cream, whipped

Spread 1 tablespoon rose petal preserves onto each crêpe, within 1/2 inch of the edge. Sprinkle 1 teaspoon chopped pistachios over preserves and top with 1 heaping tablespoon whipped cream. Roll crepes and serve garnished with remaining whipped cream and:

fresh rose petals

Makes 18 crêpes

EGYPTIAN SWEET COUSCOUS DESSERT

Among the variations of couscous this recipe from Egypt is unrivaled for the sweet-toothed palate. Serve with a cold glass of milk or a demitasse of heavy Arabic coffee.

Follow basic directions for steaming couscous (page 121), using:

1 cup couscous
2 cups fruit juice
2 tablespoons rose water
After first steaming, rub well into grains:
3 tablespoons melted sweet butter
After second steaming combine couscous with:
4 tablespoons melted sweet butter
1/4 cup each finely ground blanched almonds and pistachio nuts
Mound on serving platter and sprinkle with mixture of:
1/2 cup powdered sugar
1/2 to 1 tablespoon cinnamon
Surround with:
1 cup kufeta (candy-coated almonds)
Sprinkle with:
1/2 cup pomegranate seeds if in season
Serves 6

MOROCCAN TEA

Tea was first introduced to Morocco by British traders from the Orient in the 19th century, and has since achieved great popularity. This very sweet, minty tea is a favorite beverage, whether as a finish to a meal or for sipping in the afternoon at one of the many cafes. Spearmint has the best flavor, though other kinds of mint may be substituted.

Rinse a 4-cup teapot with boiling water. Add to the pot:
4 teaspoons green tea
1/2 cup sugar
1-1/4 cups firmly packed fresh spearmint leaves
Cover with:
4 cups boiling water
Allow tea to steep at least 3 minutes. Stir slightly and correct for sweetness. Serve hot in glasses.
Serves 6
Variation
Add fresh orange blossoms to the pot before pouring in the boiling water.

MOROCCAN SHARBAT BIL LOOZ (Almond Milk)

This is a favorite afternoon drink—cool and refreshing.

In a blender, combine until smooth:
3/4 cup whole blanched almonds
3/4 cup sugar
1-1/2 cups water
Strain well, extracting as much of the liquid as possible. Add to the strained liquid:
1-1/2 cups each milk and water
Chill thoroughly and serve.
Serves 6

BASICS

THE GREAT MOSQUE OF IKSAHAN FROM THE ALA KAPI, THE ROYAL PAVILION

LEGUMES

Garbanzo beans: Soak 2 cups garbanzo beans in water to cover overnight. Drain and place in saucepan with 4 cups water, 1/2 teaspoon salt and a few chopped onions and garlic cloves if desired. Bring to boil, cover with lid tilted, and cook over medium heat 1 to 2 hours (depending upon age of beans), or until tender. Drain and reserve liquid if recipes so indicate.
2 cups raw garbanzos make 6 cups cooked beans

Lentils: Depending upon variety, age and quality, soak overnight in water to cover if needed. Most lentils purchased here need not be presoaked. Proceed as with garbanzo beans, cutting cooking time to approximately 30 minutes. In most recipes lentils should be tender but still hold their shape. If overcooked they become mushy.
2 cups raw lentils make 4 cups cooked lentils

BULGHUR

Sauté until golden in:
2 tablespoons butter or oil
1 cup bulghur
Add:
2 cups water or stock
Bring to gentle boil, cover and cook over medium low heat 15 to 20 minutes, or until bulghur is fluffy and liquid is absorbed.
Makes 2 cups

PILAFF

Sauté until grains are translucent in:
4 tablespoons butter
1 cup long-grain rice
Stir in:
2 cups hot broth
1 teaspoon salt
Bring to boil, lower heat, cover and simmer without lifting lid 20 minutes. Remove from heat and let stand 15 minutes. Toss with fork before serving.
Makes 2 cups pilaff

Variations
Add to broth choice of following:
pinch of saffron
1/2 teaspoon turmeric or to taste
1/2 teaspoon curry powder or to taste

STEAMED RICE

Bring to boil:
2 cups hot chicken broth or water
2 tablespoons butter
1 teaspoon salt
Gradually stir in:
1 cup long-grain rice
Cover, lower heat and steam 20 minutes. Remove from heat and let stand for 10 minutes.
Makes 2 cups cooked rice

Variations
Add to broth choice of following:
pinch of saffron
1/2 teaspoon turmeric or to taste
1/2 teaspoon curry powder or to taste

BÉCHAMEL SAUCE

Melt until bubbly:
4 tablespoons butter
Add:
3 tablespoons flour
Cook and stir 3 minutes and gradually add:
2 cups hot milk, half-and-half or stock or combination
Cook and stir until smooth and thickened. Season with:
salt and white pepper to taste
seasonings called for in recipes
Makes 2 cups

BASICS

TAHINI DRESSING

Mash together:
1 to 3 garlic cloves
1/2 teaspoon salt
Blend in to make smooth paste:
1 cup each lemon juice and
    tahini*
2 tablespoons olive oil
water as needed
2 to 3 tablespoons minced fresh
    herbs such as coriander,
    parsley or dill (optional)
black pepper and cayenne
    pepper to taste
more salt if needed
Serve as dressing for vegetables
such as cauliflower and eggplant,
salads, fish, lamb dishes. Or
serve as a dip, sprinkled with
minced parsley.
*Paste made of sesame seeds
available canned in Greek,
Armenian or other Middle Eastern
shops and in some delicatessens
and markets.

CHICKEN SOUP

In large soup kettle combine:
1 stewing chicken, cut into
    eighths (for Israeli chicken
    soup, include feet, neck, and
    giblets; 4 to 5 pounds backs,
    necks and wings may be sub-
    stituted for whole chicken if
    making basic stock for other
    cuisines)
2-1/2 quarts water
2 onions chopped
2 carrots, chopped
3 celery ribs and leaves, chopped
1 parsley root, chopped
1 turnip, chopped (optional)
1 kohlrabi, chopped (optional)
6 parsley sprigs
1 tablespoon salt
10 peppercorns, lightly crushed
2 sprigs dill or thyme (optional)
Bring to gentle boil, cover and
simmer 2 hours or until chicken
is tender and meat falls from
bones. Strain, reserve chicken
meat, cool and jar stock. Refrigerate and before using, remove
fat that has congealed on top.
Save chicken meat for another
use.
Makes approximately 2 quarts

PHYLLO

Phyllo dough is almost identical
to strudel dough and is very
difficult to make at home. It may
be purchased in 1-pound packages
in Greek, Armenian and Middle
Eastern shops and many delicatessens and markets. If frozen, always
defrost overnight in the refrigerator. Well wrapped, it will keep
up to a week. The sheets, 20 to
24 in a package, dry out rapidly
and are easily broken. Depending
upon your experience with phyllo,
take out 2 to 4 sheets at a time,
reroll and rewrap the rest and
cover with a tea towel. Immediately brush each sheet with
melted butter, using a 2-inch
nylon paint brush, feather brush
or other soft brush, and stack the
buttered sheets as you work. If
sheets break, they can be mended
with another sheet. Work quickly,
following directions in individual
recipes. Always use sweet butter
when making desserts. When
cutting through prepared top
layers, use a very sharp knife or
razor blade.

DOLMAS
(Stuffed Grape Leaves)

Grape leaves are the indisputable queen of the dolmas. This hors d'oeuvre is popular throughout the Middle East, and recipes vary generally only in the herbs and spices used. Serve cold, accompanied by a chilled bowl of yoghurt.

For 1 jar of grape leaves, preferably domestic, combine for filling:
1 cup rice, soaked in cold water and drained
1/4 cup each currants and pine nuts
1 cup finely minced green onions, or
1 cup grated onion
3 tablespoons minced parsley
2 tablespoons chopped fresh dill
2 garlic cloves, minced (optional)
1/2 teaspoon allspice
salt and pepper to taste
Remove grape leaves from jar, scald with hot water and drain. Cut off stems and pat each leaf dry. Place on towel or board dull side up. Place 1 to 3 teaspoons of filling in center of each leaf. Fold end of leaf over to cover filling, fold sides in and starting at stem end, roll carefully to form a firm cylinder about 2 inches long, depending upon size of leaf. Place side by side in a heavy saucepan over a bed of leaves. Layer until all leaves are used, sprinkling each layer with:
2 tablespoons lemon juice
Add to saucepan:
1 cup water or stock
3 tablespoons olive oil
Place a heavy plate on top to weigh down, cover and simmer over low heat approximately 1 hour. Test leaves for tenderness. Remove, cool and place on large serving platter in circular or straight lines, side by side. Garnish with:
parsley sprigs
lemon wedges
Serve with bowl of chilled yoghurt.
Variations
For a Lebanese or Syrian variation, omit the pine nuts and currants. Add fresh mint and season with cinnamon. Serve with laban (yoghurt).
For a North African dolma, add a pinch of saffron to the water, or combine the water with 1/2 cup pomegranate syrup.
Persians include pistachio nuts to replace the pine nuts and a pinch of saffron mixed with the rice.

MIDDLE EASTERN CHEESES

At the present time, there are few cheeses imported from the Middle East to this country, especially to the West Coast. There are, however, some cheeses available which can be successfully substituted for those of the Middle East. An excellent substitute for the basic cheese of Palestine and Syria is Kochkaese, made in Fresno, California. A soft, salted sour milk cheese, it is usually boiled in milk or water and eaten for breakfast. Two popular pickled cheeses of Egypt are Kareish and Domiati, a soft white cheese made from whole or partly skimmed cow's or buffalo's milk. Greek or Bulgarian Feta, which is more readily available, may be substituted for these and for the pickled cheeses of Syria and Turkey.
Greek Kefalotyri or Argentine Sardo would do well for any hard or grating cheese, or Italian Pecorino Romano if a stronger, more pungent flavor is desired. The soft fresh ewe's milk cheeses of the Middle East, such as Turkish Edirne, may be approximated by the serving of the more easily obtainable Czechoslovakian Bryndza.

139

INDEX

INDEX

BIOGRAPHICAL NOTES

EVA ZANE Though Eva Zane spent four years on the actual research and writing of this book, it is the result of a lifetime of interest in the foods and peoples of the Middle East. She was raised by her Greek parents on Chicago's Halsted Street, which at that time was the hub of one of America's largest Middle Eastern communities. Among her earliest recollections are her friendships with these peoples and her fascination with their foods which has continued throughout her lifetime. Later, in San Francisco, she operated two restaurants specializing in Greek and Middle Eastern foods. In 1970, her first book *Greek Cooking for the Gods* was published, also by 101 Productions. In writing that book, she consciously eliminated all recipes from her extensive Middle Eastern repertoire that were not strictly of Greek origin, saving these for the sequel, *Middle Eastern Cookery*.

KEITH HALONEN has developed his remarkable talents and techniques with no formal training in art. The drawings for *Middle Eastern Cookery* were his first publishing commission. But subsequently he has illustrated elementary textbooks for Harcourt Brace Jovanovich, *Back to the Bike* (101 Productions) and *Echoes*, a book of poetry by James McNutt. He presently lives in Northern California devoting most of his time to his own painting.

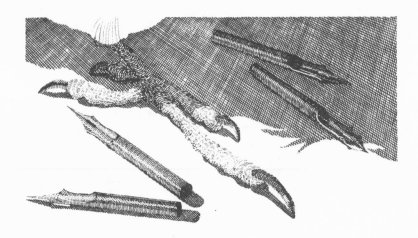